Praise for *Now Is Your Chance*

'Through the powerful practices Niyc shares in *Now Is Your Chance*, you will access a space of more joy, more fulfilment and more freedom. How amazing can your life get? Open this book and find out.'

NATALIE MACNEIL, EMMY AWARD-WINNING MEDIA ENTREPRENEUR, AUTHOR OF *SHE TAKES ON THE WORLD* AND *THE CONQUER KIT*, AND THE CREATOR OF SHETAKESONTHEWORLD.COM

'Niyc Pidgeon is a role model for millennial women worldwide, and a voice for those who crave an amazing life of success and fulfilment. She proves that absolutely anything is possible when you adapt your mindset. *Now is Your Chance* is a call to reclaim your power, grab life by the balls, and jump in with both feet. Be prepared to get inspired!'

MEL WELLS, BESTSELLING AUTHOR OF *THE GODDESS REVOLUTION*, HEALTH AND EATING PSYCHOLOGY COACH AND INTERNATIONAL SPEAKER

'Niyc Pidgeon's new book is here! In it she takes you through a powerful 30-day process (jam packed with support, tools and pep-up talks) that will set you up to live your best life, not someday in the future, but today, as in NOW!'

REBECCA CAMPBELL, AUTHOR OF *LIGHT IS THE NEW BLACK* AND *RISE SISTER RISE*

'A must read for every modern woman looking to master mindful self esteem. From social to self-talk, get the tools you need to transform negatives into truly transformational positives.'

EMMA MILDON, BESTSELLING AUTHOR OF *THE SOUL SEARCHER'S HANDBOOK*

NOW
IS YOUR
CHANCE

A 30-DAY GUIDE TO
LIVING YOUR
HAPPIEST LIFE
USING POSITIVE PSYCHOLOGY

Niyc Pidgeon

HAY HOUSE

Carlsbad, California • New York City • London
Sydney •Johannesburg • Vancouver • New Delhi

First published and distributed in the United Kingdom by:
Hay House UK Ltd, Astley House, 33 Notting Hill Gate, London W11 3JQ
Tel: +44 (0)20 3675 2450; Fax: +44 (0)20 3675 2451; www.hayhouse.co.uk

Published and distributed in the United States of America by:
Hay House Inc., PO Box 5100, Carlsbad, CA 92018-5100
Tel: (1) 760 431 7695 or (800) 654 5126; Fax: (1) 760 431 6948
or (800) 650 5115; www.hayhouse.com

Published and distributed in Australia by:
Hay House Australia Ltd, 18/36 Ralph St, Alexandria NSW 2015
Tel: (61) 2 9669 4299; Fax: (61) 2 9669 4144; www.hayhouse.com.au

Published and distributed in the Republic of South Africa by:
Hay House SA (Pty) Ltd, PO Box 990, Witkoppen 2068
info@hayhouse.co.za; www.hayhouse.co.za

Published and distributed in India by:
Hay House Publishers India, Muskaan Complex, Plot No.3, B-2,
Vasant Kunj, New Delhi 110 070
Tel: (91) 11 4176 1620; Fax: (91) 11 4176 1630; www.hayhouse.co.in

Distributed in Canada by:
Raincoast Books, 2440 Viking Way, Richmond, B.C. V6V 1N2
Tel: (1) 604 448 7100; Fax: (1) 604 270 7161; www.raincoast.com

Interior images: 181 © Rob Loxston – Rocketbox Design; all other images © Niyc
Pidgeon

For my mother, Barbara, father, Phil,
brother, Luke, and niece, Olivia.

In loving memory of Lewis McCullough, Jon Ellison,
Chris Redhead and Sara Hepburn.

CONTENTS

ACKNOWLEDGEMENTS

I stand in the deepest joy and overwhelming flow of Gratitude for the process of writing this book, which wouldn't have been possible without the support of the amazing humans surrounding me.

Thank you to Amy Kiberd, Jo Burgess, Sian Orrell, Julie Oughton, Tom Cole and Michelle Pilley at Hay House UK; Richelle Fredson and Blaine Todfield at Hay House New York; Reid Tracy, Patty Gift and, of course, Louise Hay for creating the space for so many authors to share their messages to powerfully serve so many more. With thanks to my Hay House girl gang, Mel Wells, Carrie Green and Rebecca Campbell, and my awesome editor, Sandy Draper, for helping me to bring this book to life.

Natalie Diver, my friend and Geordie sidekick here in California, thank you for your ongoing support and wizardry, and for laughing so hard at our own jokes that we cry. This entrepreneurial journey would not have been the same without you!

For my friends and room-mates Helen Jamieson, Ashley Pennington and Erin Fall Haskell, who witnessed the writing of this book from balcony and bedroom, and proposal to draft, to edit, and reassured me I wasn't going slowly insane in the process!

George Woods Baker, for your support and wisdom when I was broken, and for believing in me when I didn't.

For those of you who have allowed me to feel deep dark pain and helped me to grow. You have been my greatest teachers. All in divine time.

For the friends and loved ones we have lost, who allow us to lean to the light with deeper meaning and understanding, and a greater resolve to do more to honour your short lives and help others who are struggling: John Rankin, Lewis McCullough, Tom Maynard, Jon Ellison, Chris Redhead and Sara Hepburn.

Mum and Dad, who noticed I was a bookworm from an early age, gave me the best education because they believed in me and allowed me a long leash to reach for my dreams. I love you. My younger brother, Luke, for laughing at me and always bringing me back down to earth. I'm so proud to see you become a dad.

Thank you to each and every one of my thousands of clients. For showing up for yourselves to do the work and for the stories you agreed for me to share within the pages of this book.

For my team, who support me, my vision, mission and business daily, and who have held the space for me to create; I Thank You.

To my many coaches, and specifically those of you who have helped me recently and directly with *Now Is Your Chance* – Brendon Burchard for supporting me in finishing the book, and for being a role model who always over-delivers and raises the bar; Ryan Magdziarz for your support, strategy and for being a friend; and Zac Dixon for holding me accountable to sharing my story on stage so I can more powerfully serve.

To my mentors, whose early influence shaped my life. Wilf Gillender, for introducing me to positive thinking when you slipped those positive quotes into our passport holder back in 2005, Angie McLean for seeing and nurturing my brilliance as a presenter and entrepreneur, and Mr Fleck for helping me to overcome my fear of public speaking in high school.

To my many wonderful friends who cheer me on – you have no idea how much your words of encouragement have kept me going over the years. Most recently, Ange Loughran, Caroline Edwards and Megan Anderson, who have surrounded me with so much love and support.

Thank you to Wah Guru Khalsa and Golden Bridge for suggesting the Kundalini practice for this book.

Thank You, universe, for gifting us all, and me, with the support to be, do, create and have all we desire, and for my guides, angels and God for helping me to help you to rise.

For Sue at Rape Crisis UK, please know my eternal Gratitude for your support and helping me to find my strength, voice and heal. Maria Andersson at Onebracelet.org and United Nations Women UK for holding a space within which I've found so much alignment and power to help other women in our world, and raise awareness of the message for gender equality and ending violence to women.

And finally, for you, the reader, and for every man and woman who has struggled to find happiness – I want you to know it's available for you, it's meant for you, and it's right here within these pages and this journey you're about to embark upon. I am blessed and so are you.

With Gratitude,

Niyc xx

I am not who I am and where
I am because it was easy.

I am who I am and where
I am because it was hard.

For that I live in gratitude.

I took my difficulties and
I ran with them.

I cried.

I felt scared.

I released.

I let go.

I loved.

I healed.

And then I shone brighter
than ever before.

— Introduction —

CREATING HAPPINESS FROM THE INSIDE OUT

*'I am not what happened to me. I
am what I choose to become.'*
CARL JUNG

In our super busy, digitally connected – and yet all too often emotionally disconnected – world, it seems all too easy to focus on obstacles rather than opportunities; to turn our attention outwards in order to find solutions for problems; to worry about what's wrong with the world and what's hot on social media right Now, or to spend more time talking about other people than working on ourselves. Therefore, it seems that it's only natural that the divide between *what we do* and *how we feel* is increasing.

Happiness is the Holy Grail for so many of us, but why do we treat it like a goal or a destination that's way out in front? We want to get there, but don't quite know how. And just when we think we've cracked it, then it often seems that life throws us another challenge to deal with instead. So why can't we hold on to happiness and be happy all of the time – and what's the real goal here?

When it comes to upping our happiness quota, you'd be correct in deducing that it's not only *striving* for happiness that's the problem here, but also that happiness comes from within rather than outside us. The notion that happiness can be captured, achieved or purchased leads to disappointment when we don't manage to find it and hold on to it. The definition of happiness is much like beauty; it's in the heart and eye of the beholder. What makes one person feel happy doesn't always make everybody happy, even though statistically speaking we are more like each other than we would like to believe. Harvard psychologist Dan Gilbert shares this idea and identifies that, over time and in general, as much as we would love to believe we are unique, the same things tend to make us happy, or unhappy,[1] but it's not usually the things we think.

It might be that you believe a new car will make you happy or maybe having kids. What about that glamorous lifestyle you see the reality television stars living, or if you could only lose some weight. All of these things are put outside of ourselves and out in front, as if they are the elusive secret to becoming happy in the future.

Right now, happiness is something that's being pursued instead of being tapped into and it seems like the time has come for the perspective to shift. Where Prada bags and Louboutins might suffice for a short while, ultimately it's feelings of fulfilment and joy that will help us to feel better more of the time.

Owning up to the need for something more is the first step in doing something about it and it's clear that there is a problem here that calls for a solution. After all, we are only here on Earth for a very short time, so we may as well make the most of it.

It's true that obstacles and chaos may seem to rule, and it's easy to become so stuck in a story of what's wrong that we find it difficult to see clearly what's right. Navigating life can be confusing, frustrating and oftentimes downright scary, but through learning to make more conscious choices and raising our awareness we are able to pursue a different way. No matter whether we have to cope with a natural disaster or a daily disaster, we all have the power to make a change. This power comes from within you and Now Is Your Chance to seize it.

My journey to happy

So often it's pain and healing that serves as a catalyst for growth, and this certainly describes my journey on the way to living my happiest life.

Despite coming from a loving family, by the time I was 11 years old, I was so unhappy and fearful that I tried to take my own life in a bid to escape the bullies at school. As I grew through my teenage years, I learned to use academic achievements to feel validated and worthy, and over time started to use parties and excessive exercise as a coping mechanism to ignore what I was feeling inside. I'd become a pro at getting on with things, and I put on a brave face instead of working through the pain of my relationship breaking down, the tragic loss of friends, my parents' divorce and the trauma of being raped.

On reflection, cutting my eye open with a contact lens was the awakening I needed to start to really see and to begin to deal with the emotional roller-coaster that I'd been on. Once I'd committed to getting through to the other side, counselling and spiritual work eventually helped me to come into the light.

Where previously I was stuck with inner conflict and struggle, I was released to flourish and thrive. I became more sure on my path, found my voice, and developed a confidence and intuitive knowing that as I continued to connect in deeply, and do the work on myself, everything would be alright and even better than before.

I'll share more from my story in the following chapters but, put simply, I found that after I found out how to create and allow my own happiness, the physical ailments that had been plaguing me disappeared. I was able to release myself from past struggles and a codependent relationship, and my spark came back. After doing the healing work for myself, I left the UK for a three-month trip to Australia, from which I never returned. I launched my online coaching business, which grew quickly past six figures, and moved to Los Angeles to fulfil my own happiest life. I found my purpose, my calling and my voice: to help you become empowered, and find strength and happiness, too.

I was afforded the opportunity to go deeper into myself, to allow me to serve others from a more whole and powerful place. I won the Sage Young Business Person of The Year Award, as well as an award for breaking through barriers. With my newly discovered self-worth and focus on giving value rather than being validated, I created my dream business, serving women around the world to create more joy, personal power and unstoppable success – both within themselves and within business.

The transformative process of working from the inside out is one that this book can afford you. It will show you how to let go of the perception of fear and overcome any obstacle you're facing, but more than that, it will show you how to tap into what your definition of happiness is, and then create each and every day, no matter what curve balls come your way.

The techniques and methods that you'll discover over the coming 30 days have provided me with quantum shifts in my life and I'm excited for you to experience them, too. Now Is Your Chance to step into your power, take charge of your life and create change in the Now – because that's where your power is, not living for a tomorrow that never seems to come.

Why happiness?

Let's first begin with what happiness is and also what happiness isn't. Happiness isn't about feeling on top of the world all of the time. It's not about knowing the big secret or cracking that code and, as I said earlier, it definitely isn't a destination – despite what we might have been conditioned to believe. Rather, happiness is a journey that combines how satisfied we are with life, with how good we feel on a day-to-day basis. Instead of thinking of it as needing a key to unlock your happiness, think of happiness as the key to unlock your other desires for your life.

We know from the science that happy people are healthier, make more money, have more friends, experience better relationships and feel more fulfilled.[2-4] Happiness literally is the catalyst to begin the cascade of allowing so much more to flow. So why has happiness become cool all of a sudden? And, more importantly, why hasn't it been all along!?

A short time ago happiness wouldn't have even registered on the scale as being a priority for most people. In comparison with just 30 years ago, we have more leisure time available to us Now. We also have a wealth of knowledge and information at our fingertips that we can use to shift out of the mindset of the daily grind, and into a place of deeper feeling and meaning. The noticeable shift in energy of social media now focuses more upon aspirational lifestyle and wellbeing. The content that the world's thought leaders are sharing also calls for a greater commitment to leading wholesome, thriving lives, where we work together for the greater good. One of the most important things in life is to make our experience enjoyable and we are beginning to understand that real happiness *has* to be our priority.

Even governments have recognized the importance of happiness, as GDP is no longer the go-to measure of our standard of living, with the introduction of the Happy Planet Index, Gross National Happiness and the National Accounts of Wellbeing as measures to track our happiness and satisfaction as a collective whole. The expectation was that with higher GDP comes a better quality of life; although that has been proven to not always be the case – because, after all, how can an economy be flourishing if the population is not?

You might also expect that as incomes rise, so too does happiness; though we observe that with rising income our actual rise in happiness is correlated only up to a certain point. If money doesn't link directly to greater wellbeing, then what else can we use as a measure?

By focusing our attention and intention on creating better wellbeing, more happiness and greater life satisfaction, global leaders are more fully able to identify what's going right and what really makes a difference. The application of positive psychology (PosPsych) within policy, business, communities and you is able to support measures like GDP, to ensure that thriving communities and nations are being nurtured.

When we study the most successful leaders and the messages they are sharing, we notice that their success habits include a focus on happiness and fulfilment. Brendon Burchard talks about the power of habits, as he introduces the six high-performance habits of clarity, energy, necessity, productivity, influence and courage, and how they are powerful predictors of happiness. He created and tested the High Performance Indicator with more than 30,000 people from 195 countries to prove its validity, reliability and usefulness. It was found that the higher your score in any of these habits, the happier you'll be in life. (You can find your score in a few minutes by taking the test at www.highperformanceindicator.com.)[5] *Now Is Your Chance* is both an exploration into what you already have, with the guidance to begin to do more with these things, and create new and lasting habits as a result.

Happiness is a focal point that means feeling good naturally and even in the world of celebrity, we are noticing the trend towards living life with fulfilment, meaning and joy, instead of the reckless hedonism so common in the past. Happiness has the power to shift so many different areas of your life in to the positive that it's clear right Now, that if you make one choice, happiness should be it.

You'll notice in the last paragraph alone that I mention happiness, fulfilment and joy. I'd like to make a distinction right here, though I do go on to use the terms interchangeably through the book. Happiness is a hook – everybody would like a little more of it. Fulfilment? Deep down we know we desire it, though fewer people openly express their experiencing a lack of it... and joy. Deep joy is within you, right here, right Now. All of these emotions are available to you from within, you can feel their power rising from your heart space, when you stop, get present and connect with you.

Here's the official rundown:

- **Happiness**: The state of being happy. A mental or emotional state of wellbeing defined by positive or pleasant emotions, ranging from contentment to intense joy.

- **Fulfilment**: Satisfaction or happiness through the achievement of something desired – the meeting of a requirement or need.

- **Joy**: A feeling, source or cause of great happiness, and the highest emotional energy that allows you to attract and create at the highest possible level.

From the above definitions you'll notice that happiness encompasses both joy and fulfilment within it. So while joy and fulfilment might be experienced with greater depth than you might tend to associate with happiness alone, you both desire and deserve to experience each of these feelings and states as part of your thriving life.

What is positive psychology, anyway?

This science of happiness provides evidence-based insights into how individuals, communities and businesses thrive, and it looks at what goes right with the world, instead of what's going wrong. While only recently popularized, positive psychology is revered around the world by millions, with **70,221,060** people liking it on Facebook alone at the time of writing.

But the easiest way to understand the science of happiness is by using what's called the 'happiness pie theory' (yes, you heard me right), as shown in the diagram below:

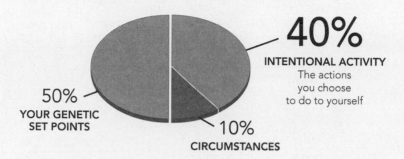

We divide the pie into sections, based upon what percentage of our happiness can be attributed to a certain element. Our genetic happiness set point is where we begin with 50 per cent of the pie, 10 per cent is effected by our environment and circumstances, and a huge 40 per cent is within our control![6] Does that surprise you? I know that when I share these statistics I tend to see a few shocked faces when people realize just how much of our happiness we can choose.

So when we complain about the traffic or the weather and we let it consume our day, we are actually doing that by choice. We are allowing our thoughts to take us in to the negative instead of focusing on what's good and feeling good as a result. It's an empowering piece of information to learn, which can in turn help us to make choices in the moment to support our wellbeing.

If you had to choose five key things to help you live your happiest life, what would they be? Long walks on the beach?

Curling up with a good book? Laughing and putting the world to rights with friends over dinner? Building a career that leaves a legacy for your children? Growing your Instagram following past 10,000 followers? Kind of, actually, yes.

Working with the 40 per cent of the happiness that's within your control (and through the science of epigenetics,[7] also now some of the 50 per cent), we are able to create a state and life that's flourishing, and thriving. For flourishing to be present you need five key things:

1. Positive emotions

2. Engagement

3. Relationships that are fulfilling

4. Meaning and purpose

5. Accomplishment

The PERMA theory of flourishing

The above five aspects make up what's known as the 'PERMA theory of flourishing' which is at the core of the 30-day happiness plan in this book. Together, these five aspects will help you to thrive and create happiness in the Now. They're also super easy to remember – which is always good!

Positive Emotions Engagement Relationships Meaning Accomplishment

'V' for Vitality can also be added to the model, to recognize the importance of physical movement. Martin Seligman, the founder of the PERMA theory and also PosPsych, shares his goal of creating a world where 51 per cent of people are flourishing. I think we can do it, do you?

I've seen the transformative power of positive psychology both through my own personal experience and also through my professional work, where it has helped to create happier people, greater productivity, rapid business growth, massive success, balanced and healed relationships, and confident, empowered people living a life that they love to live.

I hope the power of applying the teachings in this book in the Now will allow you to create action and forward motion, to serve both your happiness and your personal growth. Being present is a concept that's noted both in positive psychology and in age-old spiritual teachings such as Buddhism too, where mindfulness is recognized as the process of drawing your attention to your experience in the moment. We spend time, sometimes not so wisely, often waste it and regularly complain that we don't have enough of it! Being present and remembering that Now Is Your Chance, is something that can really help you to both take control and simultaneously help you to let go of the need for it.

Time perspective determines the frame through which we see our world and make choices. Too much living in the past, even if your memories are good, can lead to overcautiousness or rumination over things that have 'gone wrong'. Only caring about the present can lead to taking risks and addictive behaviours. And a future-oriented time perspective can lead to more success and the ability to delay gratification, but might promote such things as workaholism and burnout. The optimal time perspective for optimal function is, in fact, one that's balanced and easily switchable between all three. This means you're able to choose an appropriate time perspective when it matters – switching to a present time perspective when enjoying time with loved ones, a past positive perspective when recalling happy memories and a future perspective when executing your big vision.

I ask you to be mindful of your time perspective as you move through this book. I will be encouraging you to reflect, to project and to engage in taking action in the Now, where for the duration of this book you'll find your power.

— Using the 30-day NIYC Challenge —
GROWTH THROUGH PAIN

'Because when you stop and look around, this life is pretty amazing.'
DR SEUSS

I've briefly described how pain and healing can serve as a catalyst for growth, and over the next 30 days I'd like to share the lifehacks and PosPsych tools that have helped me to create happiness in my life, which I now share with clients around the world to help them flourish.

When I began my journey and launched my first business running motivational events, I taught textbook-style scientific theory. I knew how these teachings had helped me to feel happy, and I wanted everybody else to experience their power. At this point, though, I was still ignoring the work I needed to do on myself and so when I taught, looking back, it lacked the depth of understanding I now have.

Having been forced into the darkness to finally find my light, I was offered a new perspective on happy and a much deeper appreciation for the application of the tools during both the good times, as well as the desperate times. Working through my own process, as well as teaching these techniques to thousands of clients, has allowed me to draw together the teachings within this book, to share with you what really works.

The Now Is Your Chance action plan brings together science, lifehacks and spirit to provide a real-life road map to thriving, so that you can create purposeful, powerful, meaningful positive change in 30 days or less. Anyone can use the 30-day plan to create more happiness, but you may find it particularly helpful if you:

- Feel tired, stuck and struggling, and want a clear path to move forwards.
- Have an open mind, and are ready to be empowered to take charge of your own happiness and success.
- Are in need of some good vibes and appreciate some good fun!
- Believe in the power of the heart and the mind, and know that a higher power is always right here to support you.
- Are ready to activate your next level breakthrough and live a thriving life.

I want to put your mind at ease and help you to understand that happiness is totally doable. In fact, you already have it right Now. Letting go of the illusion that happiness is a destination is the initial step in putting this book in to action and allowing your happiest self to grow.

Now Is Your Chance is designed as a step-by-step 30-day guide, divided into three parts:

- Part I: Your Body
- Part II: Your Mind
- Part III: Your Spirit

I've designed the plan in this way because each idea builds on the previous one, and you'll enjoy some quick wins before moving on to more complex ideas and practices. The goal is to help support your growth and raise your awareness so you can experience more joy, happiness and fulfilment, and shift further into the positive, where you notice yourself feeling better more of the time. At the end of this chapter, I'll be asking you to make a note of how you feel on a really simple self-report scale.

Each day, you'll find a daily tool or teaching that you can apply into your own life, as well as real-life experiences from my life and others, take-away tips, a daily positive psychology tool or a spirit-led mantra, longer practices where helpful, as well as the latest happiness research. *Now Is Your Chance* draws from, though is not limited to, the science of PosPsych, with many of the teachings and tools having also been created, tried and tested through my own and clients' experiences.

☉ NIYC Notes ☉

Before setting out on your 30-day journey, you may want to open a file on your computer or phone, or buy a beautiful notebook that you can use to record your responses and ideas as you work through this book. I always find it helpful to store all of my work from a particular programme or coach in one place, and this will help you to refer to your notes and process more easily. It will also create a sacred space for you to find your happy.

Your highest good

It's easy to read a book and feel inspired; the important part is actually doing the work. The good news is that all of the daily practices and techniques in this book are conspiring for your highest good! You'll always feel better for using them – which means you're about to feel better every day, for the next 30 days – and beyond! I like to call these simple tools my 'NIYC Notes' and I hope that they help you to make a positive choice in a moment that can shift how you feel.

Reading the book and applying the tools daily is your 30-day immersion experience – you're surrounding yourself with these tools and teachings to give yourself a brand new kick-start in to living your happiest life. But, of course, allow these tools to become part of your every day life and you'll find that the impact of this book will extend way beyond just 30 days. These skills will help you to live your happiest life. So take the tools, find your favourites and understand which are the ones that stretch you out of your comfort zone, too. Be prepared to be uncomfortable – it's an indicator that you're growing. One of the biggest misconceptions I see is that happiness is all about thinking positive. Positive is great, but there is so much more to your journey than that.

☾ NIYC Notes ☾

You'll notice I refer to the PERMA-V criteria of flourishing at the beginning of each day. This allows you to see clearly which elements are boosted as you practise the exercises from each section. I know it's important to help you connect with why you're taking a certain action in your days and so this mini check-in tool allows you to see whether you have increased your experience of positive emotions, enhanced your level of engagement, invested in positive relationships, connected with deeper meaning and purpose, felt accomplished and become more vital as a result.

By the end of this book you'll have an increased awareness of yourself and your life. You'll understand what it is that you have been ignoring, that has been preventing you from growing and living happy. You'll have let go of the old stuff and have welcomed in the new.

More happiness might seem like a lifetime away for you right Now, but I assure you that all you need is the mindset, the tools and the right support to tap into it, feel it and let it flow. You have all three of these things right here in this book.

#NOWISYOURCHANCE: TAKE STOCK

Before we get started on the daily teachings, I'd like you to take a moment to take stock of where you are at right Now and also consider what you would like to create within the next 30 days. By setting a powerful intention, you create the space for you to grow into and fulfil it.

Grab your journal and answer the following two questions:

- How would you rate your happiness right Now, on a scale of 1–10? (Where 1 is completely unhappy and 10 is completely happy.)

- What would you love to create by the end of this Now Is Your Chance experience? For example, I would love to increase my self-report happiness score from a 4 to a 7, or, I would love to have incorporated each of the PERMA-V elements into my life.

###

Part I

YOUR BODY

Psychology is no longer a 'neck-up' discipline, as our happiness depends on the integration of body, mind and spirit, and the body is where we are starting right Now. Creating more physical sensations of happiness will not only make you feel good, but will also raise your self-awareness and self-perception.

Follow the practical ideas over the next seven days and you'll find tools that work together to positively improve your physical experience of life, quickly leading to a sense of accomplishment and boosting those all-important good feelings, so you'll gain maximum impact as you move through each day.

— Day 1 —

DROPPING G-BOMBS

*'The more you strive and search for
happiness, the more you overlook the
possibility that it is here already.'*
ROBERT HOLDEN

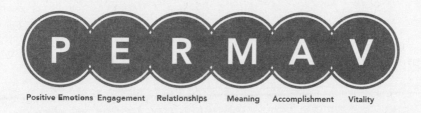

Positive Emotions Engagement Relationships Meaning Accomplishment Vitality

Gratitude brought me into positive psychology because
when I started using the simple practices, my life started
to feel better.

Gratitude is also simple, free, fulfilling and never runs out. It's
also the first practice in the book because it has a direct and
immediate effect on our physical health. The simple truth is
that each of us has something to be grateful for, whether it's
family and friends, health, the book you're holding in your
hands, or simply waking up for another day and breathing.

When we remember to feel grateful for what we have, we immediately tap into a more positive mindset, which then sends joy coursing throughout the body. This is because feeling gratitude activates the brain regions associated with the 'reward' neurotransmitter, dopamine, and the 'feel-good' hormone, serotonin. The more we practise gratitude, the stronger the neural pathways in the brain become, which in turn enhances our self-awareness and emotional intelligence.

The practice of gratitude satisfies so many of the PERMA-V criteria because it boosts positive emotions, strengthens engagement, connectedness and relationships, helps us to find a deeper meaning in life, allows us to feel accomplished, and helps us to become healthier and more vital. But why is it such a powerful intervention?

The gratitude attitude

It feels good to be thanked and giving thanks is nothing new. You've probably been encouraged to be thankful, without even realizing it, within spiritual practice, when learning manners and even by your grandmother when she told you to 'be grateful for what you've got'. What *is* new is our ability to measure the impact of gratitude and prove it works. The science of PosPsych helps us with that. For example, we know that thinking of three things we are grateful for (instead of focusing on daily hassles or something neutral) increases our positive feelings and emotions, helps us to get a better night's sleep and feel more optimistic, and helps us to develop a sense of connection with others, too. This specific intervention has also been shown to help people increase their happiness and decrease depressive symptoms for six months, and the effects last longer with consistent practice.[1]

Being grateful is described as a 'booster shot' for relationships,[2] because it fosters more romantic and non-romantic connections. The research also shows that grateful people are more likely to participate in health-promoting activities[3] and so gratitude practices can improve psychological as well as physical wellbeing.

 NIYC Notes

One of my favourite hacks to get more out of my workouts is to remind myself how grateful I am for my healthy body; it literally gives me an extra boost of energy and really keeps me going.

Gratitude practices are so simple, which means that once you get into the habit then they are easy to do every day and quickly start to create a more positive mindset. But if you need still more convincing, gratitude has also been shown to:

- Reduce stress and depression.[4]

- Build enduring levels of resilience and resourcefulness.[5]

- Enhance self-esteem.[6]

In her book *Thank and Grow Rich*, Pam Grout describes how gratitude practices clear the way for new things to flow in. This is because when we focus on what we lack and what's missing or wrong in life, it's like listening to a radio station. Because the signal is fuzzy, all you get is white noise – that's the frequency you're putting out when you try to live your happiest life from a place of need, lack and desperation. We'll be delving deeper into how all emotions have their own energy or frequency in a later chapter. All you need to know right Now is that being grateful for what you have literally allows you to cut through the crap, clear your signal, and supercharge your frequency and happiness in an instant. The following daily practice will help to get you started:

#NOWISYOURCHANCE DAILY PRACTICE: THREE GOOD THINGS

The practice of noting three good things from your day or week has been popularized as a sure-fire way to boost your happiness and strengthen your mindset. It's so simple and has such a powerful impact, but whether it's familiar to you or a brand-new thought, here follows the two-minute practice that I'd like you to follow for the next 30 days (and preferably for the rest of your life).

Pause and take a big deep breath. Now note three things that you have experienced or observed today that you can be grateful for. So, for example, you might breathe deeply and think, 'I am grateful for my mother's love, thank you, Earth, for growing food for me to eat, and gratitude to the bus driver who smiled at me today.'

That's it! But the beauty of gratitude practice is that you can do it anywhere, any time, any place (all day long if you'd like to) and there are no right or wrong answers. You're not asked to find gratitude only for certain things – gratitude is found in what's true for you.

###

Gratitude can make your life happier and more satisfying. When we feel gratitude, we benefit from the pleasant memory of a positive event in our life. And when we express our gratitude to others, we strengthen our relationship with them. But sometimes our thank you is said so casually or quickly that it's nearly meaningless. In the following reflection exercise, you can experience what it's like to express your gratitude in a thoughtful, purposeful and connected manner:

#NOWISYOURCHANCE: GRATITUDE LETTER

This proven PPI (Positive Psychology Intervention) will increase your levels of life satisfaction and happiness for a month. It only takes about 20 minutes, but the benefits are massive and immediate.

Close your eyes and take a few deep breaths. Call to mind someone who did something for you for which you're extremely grateful but to whom you never expressed your deep gratitude. This could be a relative, friend, teacher or colleague. It may be most helpful to select a person or act that you haven't thought about for a while – someone who isn't always on your mind.

Now, write a letter to this person, guided by the following steps:

- Write your letter as though you're addressing this person directly ('Dear _____').

- Don't worry about perfect grammar or spelling.

- Describe in specific terms what this person did for you, why you're grateful to them and how their behaviour has affected your life – be as detailed as possible.

- Describe what you're doing in your life Now and how you often remember his or her efforts.

- You can make your letter as long or as short as you like, but 300 words is about the suggested length.

- Once you've finished writing your letter you might choose to send or give it to the person, keep it somewhere safe, perhaps tucked into your journal, or maybe burn it and send your thanks upwards.

- Although this may not always be possible, deliver the letter in person[7] to reap maximum benefits from this practice.

I recommend you do this exercise once per month to continue to extend the powerful positive effects.

###

I practise gratitude by the minute and it's my top character strength, too (you'll be finding out what your top strengths are later in the book). Every morning I start with a grateful thought and then write at least a page in my journal for all that I am grateful for. I usually begin by saying thank you for my day, for my health, my family, friends, the pen I'm writing with, my abilities and gifts, my guides, coaches, mentors, angels, the universe and God, for allowing light to shine through me so bright every day to help other people. I like to call it a 'gratitude rampage', where things to be grateful for spill out onto the page in a flow!

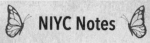

NIYC Notes

Try writing the word 'gratitude' on a sticky note and placing it where you'll see it every day – perhaps on the fridge door or on your desk – or practising gratitude when waiting in line, when in traffic or in the dentist's waiting room.

I also love to create sacred gratitude jars. At the beginning of a workshop, for example, I ask each person to write down something they feel gratitude for and place it in the jar. At the end of the workshop I read out all of the notes and love seeing the room filled with smiles. You can do this for yourself, keeping track of your gratitudes and good things by writing them on a slip of paper and placing them in a jar. When you're in need of some encouragement and a positive emotions boost, empty out the jar and read through everything in there. It's guaranteed to help remind you of all that's good... and there is so much that's good.

When my brother, Luke, picked me up from the airport recently he burst into laughter around 20 minutes into the car journey when I exclaimed, 'I'm just so grateful for...' I don't even remember what I was grateful for at the time, but he said, 'I wondered how long it would take for you to drop the G-Bomb, Niyc!' – a phrase he coined because I always say how grateful I am for everything (and I'm not about to stop Now).

Once you become accustomed to practising gratitude, you'll find that it becomes second nature and as it becomes more intuitive, the benefits get greater. You can also find and experience gratitude on a soul level, deep down inside, and in places that it might logically not make sense to find it.

When I was 24 I was raped in the back seat of what I thought was a taxi while I was on holiday in Spain. It took me two years to even tell my parents what had happened and looking back, I can see that I was experiencing rape trauma. Over-exercising and overworking were my go-to avoidance tactics. Ten months of counselling with Rape Crisis and intensive self-healing work has helped me to realize that even the darkest experiences in life can give us so much, as now I use what I learned to help others.

Writing, too, has been healing and has allowed me to reflect on what's possible when we share what scares us, and show up to being vulnerable and real. I am grateful to those people and experiences that have become my greatest teachers. Finding gratitude for that experience on a soul level, as a means to bring me to who I am and where I am today, helped me to understand the value in all experiences and what real happiness is. Gratitude has allowed me to feel powerful enough to share my experience to help you to heal, expand and grow, too.

Mindset shift

Sarah was struggling with expressing gratitude and feeling more grateful, but after we worked together and she learned how to go on a gratitude rampage, she was able to shift her mindset so she could look around and smile with gratitude:

'I started feeling, seeing and thinking of all other marvellous things in my life, at which point I began being so thankful

and grateful from sunrise to sundown, both in my meditation and in my sleep! I was grateful for my health, family, love, my husband, my twins, nature, success, my two eyes that I open every morning and being able to see the beauty in our universe, the small and big things, anything and everything! I am happier, as well as feeling healthier not only physically, but also emotionally, spiritually, psychologically and mentally. My attitude towards everything changed. My life changed! My surroundings were responding to my vibes and my energy in a different way as well by being more positive, more calm, more respectful, more caring, giving, happy, thankful and grateful.'

When seeking to live your happiest life, gratitude is key to being more conscious and aware of the happiness and joy that's already present in your life. Over time, you'll find that having a daily gratitude practice will help you to see every experience as both a lesson and a blessing. In an instant, your feelings and frequency can be transformed. So when you don't know what to do, do gratitude.

— Day 2 —
GETTING CLEAR

'The space in which we live should be for the person we are becoming now, not for the person we were in the past.'
Marie Kondō

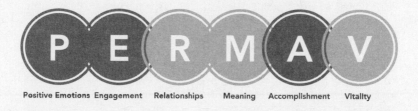

Positive Emotions Engagement Relationships Meaning Accomplishment Vitality

Yesterday, we got busy being grateful and today, I want you to consider the space where you live – both mentally and physically. Is your physical environment supporting you in creating your happiest self, and are your thoughts and actions flowing in a way that allows you to make progress?

Studies show that growing up in a chaotic environment can have a negative impact on childhood behaviour[1] and being surrounded by clutter can leave us feeling overwhelmed.[2] So in order to experience a flourishing life, we first need to create the space to allow it to happen. And while the act of letting go of a physical item you have been holding on to can evoke negative emotions and create pain in your brain, it can also release you from negative, stagnant energy. In her cult book *The Life-Changing Magic of Tidying Up*, Marie Kondo suggests that our living space affects our body and when we declutter, we literally detox the body, too!

Physically, this means getting or keeping where you live and work organized and clear; mentally, it's about clearing any stagnant energy lingering in your thoughts and letting go of any resistance towards moving forwards. We know that happiness doesn't reside in material goods; it resides within us and our experiences, and can be cultivated independently of the things we own. So let today's decluttering exercises boost our positive emotions, as well as our engagement and focus.

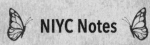

NIYC Notes

Enjoying a boost from living in an organized space doesn't have to be hugely time-consuming, as something simple like making sure you make your bed each morning is the perfect way to get started and can give you a boost of accomplishment at the start of your day.

Noticing resistance and creating space

You might notice resistance when you feel tired, or when you're scared about something, or when you're putting something off that you really should do today. Resistance is an indicator that there is something to be learned and an opportunity to grow. We all experience resistance at some point, whether it's having a challenging conversation, taking a leap of faith in business or, as in this instance, letting go of things that no longer bring us joy. It's how we respond to the resistance that makes the difference. The universe is always balanced, with light and dark, good and bad, night and day. Even physics tells us that every action has an equal and opposite reaction. It's within us and all around us, and when we start to become aware of it, we can start to let it go and create positive change.

Take a moment now to consider how you feel about change: does it excite you or worry you and make you want to shrink back and play small? Are you aware of the areas of your life where you desire change?

I know that when I ask the audiences of my talks how they feel about change, I am greeted with looks of shock and horror, which tells me how much change scares most people. But without change there is no growth, so let go of anything that no longer serves and supports your highest and happiest self. Whether it's objects or past resentments, or your daily to-dos, holding on to things that keep you in limbo between your past, present and future is a sure-fire way to halt your ride of happiness in its tracks.

Creating clarity and calm

Getting organized is super simple to do and yet it's something that's so easy to put off for another day! When we organize our physical world, we ease the pressure on our brain to remember where things are or what we need to get done. We create more ease, more allowing and more flow. So why, then, do we so often refrain from tackling things head on, and instead allow our thoughts, to-dos and more chaos to mount up? Answer – because standing still is easy, and growth requires some effort to choose to see and do things differently. If we don't change then nothing changes.

If you think about just how much 'stuff' we accumulate as we grow – both literally and metaphorically – it's no wonder that our default modality is one of worry and overwhelm instead of clarity and calm. Our lives are full, yet we don't feel fulfilled. While we move faster, do more and work harder, our brains are not actually equipped to cope with the information overload from email and friends, with Facebook notifications and work demands. It's no wonder that so many people end up feeling worn out and forgetful, like they've just managed to scrape through the day. It's time for a different approach, one that focuses more on the creation of space and the externalization of the mental overload.

#NOWISYOURCHANCE DAILY PRACTICE: BRAIN DUMP

Instead of walking around weighed down by mental baggage, choose to make space in your world by letting go of all of the thoughts that are whizzing around your mind. This five-minute daily practice will help you to gain focus, and feel more centred and grounded in your day.

Take a page in your journal or a blank sheet of paper and pen.

Set a timer for five minutes, take a deep breath and then begin writing down every thought that you have swirling around in your mind. Simply dump out all of your thoughts, feelings and ideas onto the page.

Write down anything that's inside your head, until you can't think of any more. From your shopping list to your mental memo to remind yourself to book that dentist appointment that's long overdue, commit to getting it all out of your head and onto the paper.

Then breathe!

###

 NIYC Notes

Remember that you have a choice and you always have the power to make a change in the Now. So what would you change right Now about your current physical or mental environment that would clear the clutter?

Creating space in your life for change

I know that when my environment is out of sync, I don't feel my happiest self. A study at Princeton University corroborated how our environment can negatively or positively impact our mindset, with researchers testing brain performance in organized and disorganized environments. The results showed that we are less distracted, more productive and less irritable when we live and work in an organized space.[3] So if you don't like the space where you live, then it's time to change it.

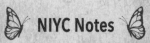

NIYC Notes

I fully believe in the power of our environment to shift our energy. Even when I was a kid I regularly rearranged my bedroom and used feng shui[4] so that my surroundings supported me better. I'm all about my space being light, bright and clutter-free, with candles, flowers and room to grow.

You might not even realize that you're feeling blocked towards your growth right Now. Perhaps you're wondering why things don't seem to be shifting in the right direction or you feel muddled and stuck. The subtleties of our energetic space can have a huge bearing on how we feel. Yes, that pile of washing might seem like a mountain that's going to take for ever to climb, but as soon as you whip up the willpower to get it done, you let go of stress and busyness, freeing you up to think about other things.

Be open to doing things differently here. Any resistance you feel towards change is likely to be the very thing that's keeping you stuck and preventing you from moving forwards. By being open to change, you also allow the option of there being a better way. Decluttering is often the first step to dropping the resistance and allowing your new normal to come in.

#NOWISYOURCHANCE:
DECLUTTER WITH THE TWO-MINUTE RULE

It's time to ask yourself if your best self in the future would be happiest in the environment you have created for yourself right Now. If the answer is no, then it's time to change it. Walking past an overflowing rubbish bin every day, sitting in a workspace that's piled high with papers or opening a wardrobe filled with clothes that you never wear (and you don't really love anymore) is symbolic of how you do the rest of your life. If your physical environment is crowded, it's likely that your mind will be crowded, too.

From now on I'd like you to use the two-minute rule, where if something takes you two minutes or less to tidy or clear away, then you do it straight away. Think gym clothes, wastepaper baskets, the plates left on the kitchen countertop instead of going straight into the dishwasher.

Now if you're a complete neat freak, then this exercise for physical decluttering probably isn't for you (though I bet you'll benefit from brain dumping those thoughts out of your mind, see page 16). If you're mostly organized, then notice the spaces where you could improve. For example, this might be your handbag, your car or the cupboard under the stairs. Beginning with one small area will give you that feeling of success – and when you create new space, you allow new energy to flow in.

###

If you want to feel happy, thriving and in flow, you don't want to be thinking about where to find your favourite pair of shoes, or be unable to think straight due to overflowing thoughts. Take this opportunity to drop the resistance, release the things that are clouding your progress and take action to declutter your life.

— Day 3 —
JUMP INTO AN
UPWARDS SPIRAL

'Bring the joy.'
BRENDON BURCHARD

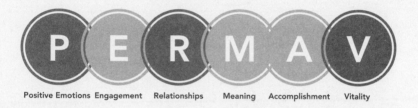

Positive Emotions Engagement Relationships Meaning Accomplishment Vitality

The work you have done over the last couple of days has started to create space for your new and happiest you. Today is about filling that space full up with goodness and letting the good vibes roll! Do you love that Friday feeling? Well, you can have it on any day of the week.

In PosPsych the study of positive emotions is one of the foundations of the science, allowing us to learn why it's good to feel better more of the time and how we can go about getting there. Our emotions don't just affect how we feel, but also how our body feels. In fact, researchers have mapped specific emotions and revealed how emotions are triggered by a stimulus that promotes a physiological response in different areas of the body.[1] So the more we experience high-vibrational emotions such as joy, love and excitement, the better our bodies feel, allowing our minds open up to a greater awareness and expansion – essentially, the more positive emotions we feel, the more we are able to feel, both Now and in the long term. We are able to see more possibility, come up with new ideas, and get creative and solution focused.[2]

We thrive on positive emotions – physically, intellectually, socially and psychologically – so the more we can expand our capacity to experience positive emotions, the more we open up to the experience of flourishing, for which positive emotions are one of the key markers.

I like to imagine positive emotions on an upwards spiral, where we can bounce from one to the next with grace and ease, filled with colour and energy and sparkles. You know that when you feel good everybody can soak up a piece of that energy, too – and, likewise, when you're not in such a good place, or someone around you is feeling blue, you can notice that their energy level can rub off on you as well.

Improve your connection to happy

Of course, nobody feels amazing all of the time – we are human, after all, and life can be stressful, but the more conscious we are about creating more positive emotions, the more we can start to have more fun. But it's not just about flooding yourself with more of what's good that's important. Rather, because negative emotions are stronger and more powerful, we need to focus on reducing the experience of the negative, while increasing the positive, too. Making a conscious effort to quit the chain of pain, get out of the downwards spiral, and replace negative feelings, thoughts and words with kinder and more supportive ones, is absolutely the place to begin. It starts by becoming aware of where your focus is and if you're moaning about the weather and traffic, or noticing a child smiling at you on the bus and allowing it to make you feel happy, too.

#NOWISYOURCHANCE: CREATING MORE JOY

This simple exercise will help you to become more aware of the sources of joy in your life:

1. First, list five things that bring you joy and increase your positive emotions. Maybe these are simple things you often overlook, or it could be something that you long to do but you've been holding off from letting yourself do. Now Is Your Chance to let go and let your positive emotions flow. For example, listening to your favourite music, calling that friend who always makes you laugh or diving into a good book.

2. Now, list five things that shift you into a negative emotional space. These are the things that drain you, or leave you feeling angry, frustrated or low. For example, spending time with that negative Nancy of a friend who just won't help herself no matter how much help you try to give, or drinking alcohol, which leads to you feeling guilty and unwell.

3. Then, choose at least one thing from the first list and commit to doing it today and every single day to bring you more joy. Then, choose something from the second list you'll do less of, so you rebalance your happiness ratio and make joy your new normal.

Discovering what brings you joy

For me, one of these simple pleasures is in music – the healing force of the universe. I spend every morning listening to a theme tune and I always dance! Now for somebody who used to feel awkward trying to dance, it's a huge breakthrough that this is one of my loves now. I love the way music makes me feel, the way it can remind me of a moment, time or place, and the power it has to change my mood and focus in an instant.

If you're feeling in a funk, and you want to raise your vibration and get things done, then music is the way to do it. In three minutes flat you can completely change your state! As humans we are made up of energy, frequencies and vibration, and as we move through different emotions, we operate at a different energetic frequency. Sound is incredibly healing, allowing us to rebalance, transform and raise our vibration from a cellular level. Have you ever experienced the gong at the end of your yoga class and left the studio feeling high? You're connecting to the frequency of the sound, and allowing it to take you onwards and upwards.

#NOWISYOURCHANCE DAILY PRACTICE: RAISE YOUR VIBRATION

Raise your vibration using sound, because when you get on the frequency and feel positive emotions like excitement, joy and love, you're vibrating more highly, and you're connected in with the flow of happiness, creativity and abundance.

Each day, take five minutes out of your day to turn on your favourite song and dance like nobody is watching, or use my Frequency of Joy Meditation found at: www.niycpidgeon.com/resources

###

Today, I'd like you to notice how you're starting to subtly shift into the positive by focusing on what's good. The fun factor allows more positive to flow and so I'm giving you permission today to choose something fun. Go and do something that you really love – play music, have that dance party or call that friend who always makes you laugh until your sides hurt. So often our own happiness falls by the wayside. Today, you're making fun and happiness a priority. Sound good?

— Day 4 —

MOVE YOUR BODY,
MOVE YOUR MOOD

*'Not exercising is the equivalent
to taking depressants.'*
TAL BEN-SHAHAR

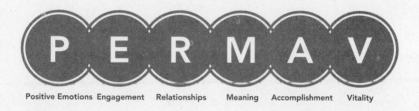

Positive Emotions Engagement   Relationships   Meaning   Accomplishment   Vitality

Yesterday we talked about creating more positive emotions and exercise is one of the biggest mood boosters on the planet. We also looked at how resistance and tension can be likened to the struggles and hurdles that we experience in life – it might feel like the hardest thing at the time, but you know that it's only temporary and you'll feel proud of yourself when you get through it.

This is why today's focus is on getting physical, because your daily workout can provide a metaphor for wider life. Just as you push your fitness out of the comfort zone, you also up the level of your relationships and career. But PosPsych studies also show that physical activity can help to make life more fulfilling.[1] In other words, giving that little bit extra at the end of your spin class, or holding that yoga pose for one second more than you think you can, is representative of how you do life. Choose to make your struggle your strength and make moving your body meaningful.

Whether you love to dance, walk, run or practise yoga, physical activity is a form of self-expression and there is something for everyone to enjoy. Working out needn't be a chore and it should be just like brushing your teeth – an essential part of your day that's filled with benefits, too.

Game-on mode

When asked what 'one piece of advice he would give' for improving productivity, global entrepreneur and thought leader Sir Richard Branson replied, 'Work out'. That might seem to be a strange reply, but having a daily workout can give us four extra focused, productive hours in the day.

Exercise is described as a 'stellar' positive psychology intervention,[2] which prepares the brain for the intake of information,[3] switches us into 'game-on' mode, and enhances our positive emotions, self-efficacy and productivity throughout the day. As well as exercise giving you that feel-good high after you finish it, as your brain releases endorphins, your levels of a protein called Brain Derived Neurotropic Factor (BDNF) also become more concentrated. BDNF triggers chemicals that promote brain health, rejuvenate brain and muscle tissues, and activate the production of new neurons in the hippocampus. In addition, it helps you to maintain your memory, perform at your peak and alleviate depression and anxiety.

A study into the brains of rats looked at the effect of exercise on neurogenesis and whether aerobic, HIIT (high-intensity interval training) or resistance training resulted in the building of new neurons. After 6–8 weeks, the study found that prolonged aerobic exercise improves brain function and protects against cognitive decline.[4]

Why we resist

So why do we view exercise as being so hard? Usually, it's because we fail to make it FUN. Positive experiences are vital to help you stick to an exercise regime and maintain the behaviour change over time.[5] We build exercise up in our minds so much that when it comes to the end of the day and we are supposed to be going to the gym, there's a whole pile of excuses. Instead of thinking of it as your time for loving yourself and your body, you have to climb a mental mountain to find the motivation even to make it to the gym, never mind complete your workout.

This was certainly true for me, as I hated sport at school and was bullied in PE lessons. I would swing to hit the ball in rounders only to be caught out and I used to stand at the end of the hockey field with my friend Rachel, chatting away in the freezing cold, hoping the ball didn't come our way. So how did I end up spending a decade as a personal trainer, studying sport science at university, having a load of half marathons under my belt and making the psychology of physical activity the focus for my Masters degree thesis? It's because I found something that I loved and chose to pursue it. A lesson for all of life and not just the way we work out.

Spending time in Australia as a teenager, I realized that fitness wasn't always about sport. I started to run. I found that running was something that really chilled me out, it allowed my thoughts to flow and I could see myself progressing. I soon started to love the way that I felt and turned my thoughts to how I could make this new-found love a part of my career and life. Fitness provides us with so much that can help us to thrive – positive emotions, engagement and challenge, and the opportunity to socialize, find a purposeful pursuit and feel a sense of accomplishment while doing so.

 NIYC Notes

If you're sitting there unable to think of one single activity that gets your pulse racing, then you might like to think back to your childhood and what you enjoyed then. Perhaps you loved roller or ice skating, dancing, swimming, playing tennis or baseball, or going to the park for a kick about. Let what you used to do inspire you to create the perfect workout for you.

Life in motion

Moving your body means moving your mind and our bodies are designed to 'do'. Seeing the transformative effect of physical exercise for energy, confidence, mood and productivity makes it no surprise that moving your body is accepted as one of the major keys in leading a flourishing and thriving life.

A life in motion affords us so much that's good. It's not enough to think of exercise as something you 'must' do – it's your non-negotiable highway to happiness. If I told you that there was a process that only required a few minutes of your time each day that would allow you to be more productive at work, have better relationships, reach your goals faster, feel better, look better, increase your self-esteem, sleep better AND have better sex, and the process was completely free… would you be prepared to try it? Of course you would! And that's exactly what exercise is! It's literally a low-risk investment that guarantees a return! So no more putting off until tomorrow the things that you can do today.

The general rule is that some exercise is good and more is better, with some of the positive effects associated with being active including:

- Enhanced self-esteem

- Greater sense of wellbeing

- Improved brain function

- Greater sense of flow

- Reduced incidence of cancers, risk of diabetes, high blood pressure and obesity

- Enhanced stress management

- Increased energy levels

- Greater focus and mental clarity

I love that feeling of energy, strength and complete clarity of thought that you get after a workout. Everything seems all right with the world and you can focus more easily on what's possible. Moving your body should be part of your daily life – and Now is your time to start. Today is the day when you say, 'Dayum, I feel good,' and you know it's because you got moving. Just 20 minutes of walking is enough to switch on your brain and prepare it for the intake of information.

#NOWISYOURCHANCE DAILY PRACTICE: 10-MINUTE WORKOUT

Choose a type of exercise that you enjoy and do it for at least 10 minutes today. This might mean taking a brisk walk, going for a swim, playing Acroyoga in the park, or visiting www.niycpidgeon.com/resources to try out my super simple 10-minute workout.

###

Great things do not come to those who live inside their comfort zone. Nor do they come to those who sit on the sofa thinking about moving! So take action. Believe me, both your body and your brain will thank you for it!

— Day 5 —

NOURISH TO FLOURISH

*'Happiness is the biggest yet best
kept beauty secret of all.'*
MEL WELLS

Positive Emotions Engagement Relationships Meaning Accomplishment Vitality

A dmit it, you're feeling great after yesterday's workout. Take a moment to look at your reflection and feel really happy about all the good things that exercise will bring to your life. Today's focus is the natural partner to moving your body – and that's how you fuel it.

As a green-juice wielding, plant-powered female entrepreneur, I need lots of energy so that I can live life to its fullest and feel fabulous doing it. Positive psychology teaches us that food has a direct effect on our mood and a recent study found that eating seven servings of vegetables a day impacts how we feel in the days following.[1]

Our bodies and minds need nutrients to function effectively, which is why it's important to focus on adding foods that are rich in happiness-boosting vitamins and minerals, such as calcium, chromium, folic acid, iron, magnesium, omega-3 fatty acids, vitamin B6, vitamin B12, vitamin D and zinc.[2] These elements are essential for creating happy bodies and brains, and when you focus on your eating behaviour and fuelling your own thriving via the food you eat, you give yourself the best chance to optimize how your body looks and feels each day.

As well as nourishing your body, food also offers us an opportunity to refuel mind and spirit, as we can choose to eat consciously – being kind to the Earth and ourselves.

 NIYC Notes

If you were told that you had a life-threatening disease that required you to become your healthiest self, how would you choose to eat? If your diet is a million miles away from this right Now, then maybe it's time you made some choices that move you in the right direction. Don't think about it as making a huge lifestyle change, but rather small shifts each day to create change. This is because it's what you do today and every day that will make a difference to tomorrow.

Small shifts in the right direction

We are gifted with one body and one mind, and we have a huge opportunity to make the most of these gifts. I started my exploration into conscious eating with the intention that knowledge is power. The more I could learn about food, and how it can support us in preventing disease and feeling our best, the more I could make an informed choice of how I want to live – and then help others to do the same.

I fully believe that food is one of the greatest pleasures in life (and those who know me well will attest that I am a walking restaurant guide and love the theatre of going out to eat!). Working as a personal trainer – and even more so as a teenage girl who hated every part of her body except for her wrists – I've learned the value in loving food, loving yourself and making food choices that allow both passions to coexist.

Where your happiness is concerned, it's clear that food provides an opportunity to both increase your experience of positive emotions, joy and self-love, or rapidly deplete it. One of the quickest ways to slide downwards into self-loathing is to beat yourself up about your body, your diet or something you wish you hadn't just eaten. When it comes to nourishing your body, you need to take care of what you eat, as well as how you think and feel about what you eat. Mindset and actions together is what will help you to achieve results.

#NOWISYOURCHANCE DAILY PRACTICE: BRING YOUR MIND TO THE TABLE

Today's daily practice is about becoming aware of how you're nourishing your body and giving yourself a little dose of self-love at the same time.

Each time you eat, take in the sight and smell of your food. Consider how lucky you are to be able to choose what you eat every day and to have such an abundance of nourishing food available.

By pausing and getting present, we begin to break the pattern of stressed-out eating, giving our wellbeing a little boost, too.

You might also like to offer up an affirmation of gratitude inside your head before eating, perhaps by saying, 'I am grateful for this food that gives me life and supports my growth. I am grateful for this opportunity to nourish myself and practise self-love in this way.'

Intentional eating encourages compassion, self-love and nourishment from the inside out.

###

Foods to boost your mood

Foods that are known to improve your wellbeing are, of course, fruits and vegetables, as well as water, coffee, chocolate and wine (in moderation) – which I'm sure will make you feel happy just hearing this! The age-old adage of 'everything in moderation' rings true here. A small amount of high-quality coffee, dark chocolate and red wine are said to be supportive of good wellbeing, but too much is said to lead to dehydration, anxiety, headaches, sleep disturbances, feelings of guilt, and physical and psychological decline.

NIYC Notes

If you struggle to eat your quota of fruit and veg each day, then consider adding a green smoothie to your day. I've included my favourite recipe below – it's super quick to make, and contains those seven servings of fruit and vegetables that are known to boost your mood. I like to drink mine in the morning to supercharge my day.

Simply blend the following ingredients together:

- 2 cucumbers

- 400g/2 cups pineapple chunks

- 30g/1 cup spinach (or kale if you prefer)

- 100g/1 cup celery (chopped)

- Juice of 1 lemon or lime

- 240ml/1 cup water

- Pinch of salt

- BONUS addition: 1 scoop of green powder for a super-boost

When we eat well we are able to give our amazing bodies the love and respect that they deserve. We have the choice and power to support and love our bodies every single day, through how we think, how we sleep, how we choose to move and how we eat. You're filling your body up as a fuel tank that carries you through your day. You can fill yourself up with positive energy, nourishing food, happiness, health and love. Though at the same time your fuel can be depleted by stress, negative energy, poor nutrition and inactivity. The result, if we are not careful, can be an unhealthy body, a lowered immune system and a less than optimal state of being.

Remind yourself of the constricting nature of negative emotions and the next time you notice you have made a poor choice with a meal, choose to find gratitude for the ability to make a positive choice with your next one – and then do it! Guilt and self-loathing have the power to keep you stuck in a repeating cycle, so don't beat yourself up if you make a poor choice, simply focus on making a positive one next time. Remember that Now Is Your Chance to make a change, and feel the power of the moment and your opportunity to fill up your metaphorical fuel tank at every meal.

 NIYC Notes

I encourage you to adopt a mindful way of eating today, by downloading a food and mood tracker from www.niycpidgeon. com/resources. This simple tool can help you to track what you eat and how you feel, so you can choose to do more of what helps you to feel good and less of what doesn't.

Over the years I've tried many different diets and eating plans. I've been vegan, vegetarian, pescatarian, been on a juice cleanse, a smoothie diet, eaten only soup or apples for days, I've eaten pizza and pineapple, substituted alcohol for food, taken slimming pills and supplements, tried thermogenics, protein shakes and eaten one big meal a day or six snacks a day, and everything in between. Do you know what worked? All of it and none of it, for different reasons and in different ways. But what has endured over time for living life as my happiest and healthiest self are a few basic principles, which I encourage you to include in your life in a way that feels best for you.

#NOWISYOURCHANCE DAILY PRACTICE: EVERYDAY PRINCIPLES OF HEALTHY EATING

Take a look through the list below and choose just one new way to nourish yourself daily. Get intentional about this practice and make it a new positive habit, and then return to the list and add something more. Making small changes allows you to feel accomplished and helps you to see the change you're creating step by step.

Drink water on waking: Drink a large glass of warm water with a squeeze of fresh lemon or lime. Adding a pinch of pink Himalayan salt is even better than drinking it plain, because it helps to improve your mineral balance and replenish your adrenals. While citrus fruits are acidic, they become alkaline once ingested and so shift your pH balance closer to where it needs to be.

Drink a shot of aloe vera drinking gel: This is an acquired taste, but is fantastic for your sleep, skin and energy levels. Aloe vera is a superfood that has more than 12 different health benefits and it's something I include in my happiness toolkit every day.

Eat a protein-rich breakfast: Eating protein in the morning regulates your hormones and blood sugar, as well as your appetite, which means you stay fuller for longer. My favourite is a bowl of quinoa with blueberries, seeds, goji berries, almond milk, almond butter and vegan protein powder.

Drink a green juice or smoothie per day: This is a great way to get your seven servings of fruit and vegetables into your day, packing your body and diet with nutrients. I make the green smoothie I shared with you earlier (see page 37) and use Green Vibrance powder, which you can find at my store: www.optimallyou.com

Choose healthy snacks: Side-step the sugary carbs and snack on a few almonds, some vegetable sticks with hummus or a protein shake with almond milk, and drink herbal teas, too. Sugar can spike insulin levels, diminish brain function, and lead to obesity and diseases such as diabetes, which impair brain function further.

Eat as nature intended: Choose the most natural versions of your food possible, which are nutrient dense and good to your body. This means going for a potato instead of French fries or a full-fat yoghurt instead of a low-fat chemical-filled one. The aspartame and sweeteners in low-fat foods can wreak havoc on your mood, and have even been linked with diabetes and seizures.

Treat yourself: Once or twice a week choose the foods or dishes you love, whatever that may be – and really enjoy the experience. This is so important for your self-care (and your sanity), and I really believe in surrounding your food with positive energy, instead of dropping down into low-level constricting emotions such as guilt.

Eat mindfully: Take a few deep breaths before you eat and avoid eating on the go, because a calm state and being present without distractions supports effective digestion, adds enjoyment to eating and means you're less likely to overeat.

Enjoy your food: Share food with friends and say thank you silently or out loud before you eat.

Think of food like energy: Before eating, ask yourself how much life force each food you choose contains. Choose high-vibrational foods, eating mostly plants (or at least five to seven servings of plant-based food a day) so that you boost your energy.

Focus on making positive choices: Move towards your most ideal way of eating by taking one positive step and then another. Choose to include more good things and the stuff that isn't so good for you will naturally fall away. Keeping a positive focus and not allowing yourself to fall into the indulge-regret cycle can keep your body healthy and your mindset strong.

Be mindful of your diet danger zones: Maybe for you it's pastries at break time, a six-shot latte at lunch or donuts while you're driving. But one thing is for sure, you've probably been lying to yourself for a little too long and it's time to start making some positive shifts. Once you know where your danger zones lie, you're more able to plan ahead with new healthy habits.

###

Making conscious food choices can allow you to nourish and flourish. Make choices that are in support of your best self and ideal health that give you boundless energy to take on the world. Lacking energy is one of the most common complaints today and with that comes a lack of willpower, poor mindset and behavioural choices, and the likelihood that you feel like your happiest life has gone right out of the window. When you're in an energized state, with nutrition that supports you, so much more is possible. Choose that today.

— Day 6 —

ACT AS IF

*'How you do one thing is how
you do everything.'*
ANON

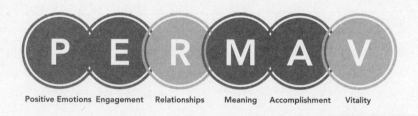

Positive Emotions Engagement Relationships Meaning Accomplishment Vitality

W e've covered a lot of ground so far – big changes in a short space of time, huh? Now take a moment to imagine what it would be like if you were living your happiest life right Now. How would you be feeling and how would you be behaving? Are you actually being the person who you intend to become? You're learning some powerful techniques within the pages of this book, but you're also working with small nuances and mindset shifts that might not be so immediately obvious.

Today, I want you to consider where you might notice a divide between who you desire to be and who you're being right Now.

I want you to notice where your actions are out of alignment with the way you think and feel, and where they are out of integrity with your values.

If you're not doing what you say you'll do, then it's time to bring your goals inside. To bring your goals, dreams and best self inside of you, and to start really living them, right Now.

Showing up

In a session with my client Emma recently, we spoke about her fantastic organizational skills and assertiveness. She observed she had demonstrated these in her relationship and family life, and also within her professional law career, but she wasn't showing up as powerfully within her business. When she illuminated this gap, she was able to commit to being the person she intended to become and allow herself to grow even more quickly than she already was.

The time is ripe and it's Now

What have you been putting off for tomorrow that you really could do today? Your best self isn't being created next week! It's the small incremental steps and changes that add up to being your best self in the Now. Stop letting yourself down! Start building yourself up. Right Now, I invite you to be the person you intend to become. It's no good waiting to be your happiest you in a year's time – your power is within yourself and within the Now.

When you think of who you desire to become in the future, what qualities do you see in your future self? Much like connecting in with your emotions in the Now, I want you to connect in with those qualities Now, too. If the happiest version of you is somebody who works out, then go and work out! If the happiest version of you makes a point of saying hello to everybody she meets, then make that happen, starting right Now. When you decide to be the person you intend to become, you start to understand that you already are that person, that it's possible to feel different in an instant.

#NOWISYOURCHANCE DAILY PRACTICE: CHECK IN

We'll be delving into meditation and the power of mindfulness in Part III but, put simply, it's focusing on the now (the present moment), and it's a fantastic way to heighten your awareness of who you are in relation to who you intend to become. So the daily practice I would like you to add to your schedule today involves checking in with yourself throughout today and simply noticing if you're acting 'as if'.

Become mindful by asking yourself, 'What would the happiest version of me be doing in this situation right Now? What would the happiest version of me be doing with this thought or this feeling or this emotion right Now?'

Through this regular checking-in practice, you'll find that you start to build better habits and hold yourself accountable at a higher level.

###

The magic of energy and intention

For me, happiness is always an exercise in self-awareness. The ability to detach from a thought, feeling, emotion, situation or environmental stimulus, and at the same time be completely present and aware of what is, and what might be. In that moment you can choose your next response. You can assess whether you're living as if, or whether your intentions and reality are right Now worlds apart. I'd like you to ask yourself the following question: When you feel fulfilled and experience life as your happiest self, what do you see yourself doing?

Quite often, acting as if will involve making changes to your actions, environments and who you're surrounding yourself with. Your environment should allow you to feel good and flourish. If you ask yourself this question right Now, could you answer with a resounding 'YES'? You're always responsible for the energy you bring to a situation, and you're also responsible for the energy you surround yourself with in your experiences and activities. You'll notice a theme of accountability coming through this book, and I strongly encourage you to show up for yourself in the places and with the exercises that may make you feel a little uncomfortable. That's where the magic is going to happen, my friend. The energy and intention you bring to everything you do will allow you to garner a greater depth of experience and positive expansion throughout this 30-day journey together. Ask yourself, are you acting, being and seeing as your happiest self right Now? It's a big wide world out there and there's just one thing to do: be better only than the current best version of you.

#NOWISYOURCHANCE:
IDENTIFY YOUR ENERGY SOURCES

Draw up a table in your NIYC journal like the one shown below. Now list the major activities and experiences in your life. Consider which experiences are adding to or draining from your energy and forwards motion, and what you would be doing differently if you were acting as if.

Activity	+ Energy	– Energy	'As If' Action
Cooking dinner for family	Creates connection with kids	Arguments and stressful environment	Focus on asking every member of the family for one good thing from their day, and commit to being the person who radiates and holds the positive space for others
Spending time with friends	Laughing about old times	Gossiping about other people	Commitment to keep the conversation positive and ideas focused
Exercising in the gym	Doing something is better than nothing	Dislike your reflection, give up after 10 minutes and just play on your phone	Minimum of five sessions per week, with the intention of being a high-performing human

###

When you act 'as if', you send a signal that says you're committed to being the highest expression of you and when you take mindful steps towards this end, it allows you to feel accomplished. You also deepen your sense of meaning around what it means for you to live your happiest life. By getting that out in front, you become more engaged with the process and move into the space where you're acting as if you already are your happiest self, which makes you feel good.

DO WHAT YOU DO BEST

'Focus on your strengths. There are better starters than me, but I'm a strong finisher.'
Usain Bolt

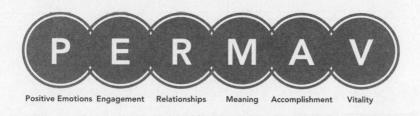

Positive Emotions Engagement Relationships Meaning Accomplishment Vitality

Yesterday we looked at acting 'as if' and today's practice is another act of self-love, because we'll be searching out our strengths and celebrating them. Armed with this knowledge, I want you to feel empowered from the inside out.

You may already know what you think you're good at, but rather like knowing makes us happy, it turns out that we are also poor predictors of what we are good at, too! PosPsych encourages us to play to our strengths and virtues, and focus on what's going well, instead of what's wrong.

For me, our strengths are inherently embodied and perceiving them as physical attributes – radiating outwards from our heart space – can help us to understand the association of character strengths with the body.

Celebrate you

To start to recognize strengths, I'd like you to spend a little time thinking about what's getting in the way of standing in your power, shining bright with your brilliance and shouting from the rooftops, 'I am amazing!'

While growing up we are told not to blow our own trumpets and to 'stop showing off'. This contributes to so many people feeling comfortable with accepting less or thinking of themselves as less than, or not good enough. Humility and modesty both have their place, but these virtues can get mixed up with being too self-deprecating or even become a form of self-protection. I see people all of the time, putting themselves down, not celebrating themselves or not being able to accept a compliment graciously.

We need to celebrate more: our lives, our opportunities, our strengths. We can celebrate from a space of being centred and grounded without being arrogant or showing off. But where does sense of self start and lack of self end? Are you selfish if you celebrate your strengths? Hell no!

Consider what's important and where your values are held. If you want to live your happiest life, then letting go of the reluctance to celebrate yourself will be key in you experiencing the full benefit of today's lesson.

Now it's not like being in an appraisal or a performance review here and you're not being judged on what you're not good at or need to improve, either. Imagine if every time you wanted to complain about something you're struggling with or not good at, you were able to check yourself and instead focus on what you're good at, and do some more of that instead. Excellent news... Now you can!

Values in action

Remember back in school when you were expected to be good at everything and work harder on your weakest subjects in order to bring everything up to the same level. Well, in the big wide world and PosPsych it's slightly different... do more of what you do best, have more fun doing it and you'll actually see better results.

We are celebrating your strengths and allowing you to be in that space of celebration every single day. You're about to work out what you're good at, own that knowledge and then put it into action to help you thrive.

Working to your strengths helps you to become stronger and more successful, reach your goals more quickly, experience more joy, and increase and sustain your wellbeing. Once you know what you're good at, you can exercise your strengths daily and with great enjoyment.

We all have the same range of character strengths within us, but each of us will use them to a varying degree. The Values In Action (VIA) classification identifies 24 strengths that sit within six categories of virtue, which are:

- **Wisdom and Knowledge:** Creativity, Curiosity, Judgement, Love of Learning, Perspective

- **Courage:** Bravery, Perseverance, Honesty, Zest

- **Humanity:** Love, Kindness, Social Intelligence

- **Transcendence:** Appreciation of Beauty and Excellence, Gratitude, Hope, Humour, Spirituality

- **Temperance:** Forgiveness, Humility, Prudence, Self-regulation

- **Justice:** Teamwork, Fairness, Leadership

Strengths bring fulfilment, as they can be measured, strengthened and developed through using them more. The VIA can help you to identify which are your top five character strengths and you can then choose to work on these strengths so they become supercharged. What's awesome about strengths is that everybody has them, and so even just knowing this and working out your top five brings you great satisfaction.

#NOWISYOURCHANCE DAILY PRACTICE:
PUT YOUR STRENGTHS TO WORK

Knowing your strengths can give you a huge boost in confidence, clarity and motivation. My top five are gratitude, humour, hope, forgiveness and appreciation of beauty and excellence.

Now it's your turn. Complete the 'VIA Strengths Assessment' at www.viacharacter.org and find out what your top five strengths are. The assessment will take around 15 minutes to complete.

When you know what your top five strengths are, you can use them in your life daily to help you feel happier, stronger and more successful. Take your top five strengths and come up with a creative way to use them in your daily life.

 NIYC Notes

I stick my own strengths up on my noticeboard so I can see them every day and consciously notice opportunities to strengthen them. I would suggest you do this, too – like any of the tips and tools here, you need to put them in to action to create a change.

NOWISYOURCHANCE: BEING CREATIVE WITH YOUR STRENGTHS

To get the most out of your application of your strengths it's important that you use them creatively, which means coming up with something new.

So, for example, gratitude could be practised creatively by sending thank-you cards to clients. Humour might come through broadcasting a Facebook Live and sharing a funny story with your community. Hope might be exercised through working on a vision. Gratitude might be practised through writing a gratitude letter (see Day 1, page 7). Appreciation of beauty and excellence could be strengthened through considering three things you love about somebody and sharing the compliment with them.

Now it's your turn…

Using your strengths will help you to live your happiest life as it satisfies all six of the PERMA-V elements. As you uncover and begin to work with your strengths, you'll find that you feel better and experience satisfaction through knowing you're doing something good. You deepen the meaning in your life, and are able to connect with people and build relationships more easily. Because you're consciously choosing to use your strengths, you're more mindfully engaged, energized and vital.

Summary: Daily Practices for Your Body

In the past seven days you've been working with practices and interventions that promote the embodiment of joy and flourishing. Here's a reminder of the daily practices you should be using to keep you on track:

- Three good things

- Brain dump

- Raise your vibration

- 10-minute workout

- Bring your mind to the table

- Check in

- Put your strengths to work

Part II

YOUR MIND

Did you know that you can enhance your experience of happiness and flourishing simply by making a commitment to working on your emotional wellbeing, mindset, vision for your future and self-acceptance? This is because happiness is a state of mind and therefore a choice that we can make each day. By becoming more self-aware of your thoughts you'll begin to see that it's not what happens that matters, but how you choose to respond to it. This is because it shapes the way you feel and how you experience life.

In Part I, we considered happiness in relation to physiology and the body. Part II will guide you through practices to help you shift into a more positive psychological space.

— Day 8 —

DON'T BE A BOTTLE, BE A SIEVE

'Beautiful flowers blossom in adversity.'
NIYC PIDGEON

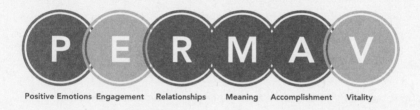

Positive Emotions Engagement   Relationships   Meaning   Accomplishment   Vitality

I n Part III we'll explore how helping others helps us, too. But for now I'd like you simply to consider the act of sharing and how it helps us to connect. By being vulnerable, we become more real and are able to heal. It's difficult to be vulnerable, though, and instead we often bottle up feelings, hurt and pain.

The problem is that all too often we think that by putting a brave face on our hurt and pain, we are being strong, and that nobody wants to hear our shit. But the reality is that we are all humans, here to help each other and learn from each other. The more real we can be, without complaining, blaming and being in victim mode, the more we can support each other where we need it.

Choose to do things differently

I've had some friends who seemed distant but then later revealed they'd been struggling with bulimia, and other friends who took their own lives because the struggle was too much for them to cope with. It's both painful and empowering to be in a position to influence change, but there's one thing I know for certain – struggle manifests for a greater good. No matter how unfair, unexplainable or downright tragic something is, we have the choice to do something good because of it. With every loss of a friend, I've become more resolute about having a huge voice in our world, to help those who are struggling in silence to be helped and be heard. When the common voice is one that's encouraging to those experiencing pain, and there is guidance on where to find support, solace and help, we can at least know we are taking a step in the right direction of making a difference.

The journey towards creating a happier life is not always going to be easy and sometimes you might want to give up. But when you attach a different meaning and allow experience to flow through you rather than consume you, you can begin to understand the real power of speaking up. When I was struggling I found it helpful to confide in one or two people who helped me to feel safe. I was able to share how I was feeling and because I knew someone was there to listen, I felt supported and encouraged that things would start to feel better again. Choose to focus on what you can control and let go of the things you can't. You'll start to see that letting go is actually incredibly powerful and empowering, and can help you to manage worries and anxieties related to projecting forwards into the future. Focus on the Now, which is where you'll find your strength.

Even when things feel tough, you always have the power to choose your next positive action. This might mean speaking up, doing something differently, asking for guidance through meditation or finding faith in spiritual practice. Armed with the tools inside these pages, you're never going to quit and as Winston Churchill said, 'If you're going through hell, keep going.'

#NOWISYOURCHANCE: LEARNING TO SHARE

Use the following self-inquiry exercise to help you start to recognize where you're bottling up your feelings and what you need to support you. Self-expression is a work in progress, and you'll feel more empowered each time you practise saying something you were previously afraid to say. Even getting aware, and observing your thoughts and feelings, then getting them down onto paper is going to help you to get out of your head and begin the process. Choose to let go of the outcome and remember, when you come from cause and speak your truth, you're making a positive step to improve.

- What negative thoughts or worries do you notice going around and around in your head?

- What would you love to be able to speak up about or share?

- Who could you share with in a safe space where you'll feel most supported?

- When can you do this?

Allowing your emotions

The more you can observe and allow your emotions without feeling attached to them, the greater your ability to process your feelings and move forwards.

I like to consider my emotions as just 'interesting' emotions and my thoughts as 'interesting' thoughts. By letting go of self-judgement in this way, you can be kinder to yourself, direct forgiveness to yourself and others, and find new strength and learning through non-attachment. You can practise this at home by sitting in silence, focusing on your breath or in meditation (see also Day 23, page 171), simply noticing the thoughts that pass through your mind, without judging them. You just notice them float in and float away. Similarly with experiences, you can practise non-attachment by understanding that all things are temporary and shall pass. This allows you to live more in the moment and savour the Now.

#NOWISYOURCHANCE DAILY PRACTICE: EXPRESS YOUR TRUTH

Today, I would like you to use the following affirmation to support you in expressing your truth:

> *'As I share my truth I empower others to help themselves, and heal both myself and them.'*

###

 NIYC Notes

I worked with storytelling coach Bo Eason recently, who works to help others to capture their story in a single sentence and tell it on stage from an empowered place. I found his practical techniques really useful and you, too, might find the following practice can help. Think about a painful story from your life. How could you share it with others, so they can see how you have worked through your challenges and how they can, too?

What would it look like if you chose to share your struggle from a place of desire so you could come out of the other side shining? How would that feel different to complaining about it or resigning yourself to absolute disaster, failure and no hope?

I used to be terrified of sharing any part of me and so I'm not teaching today from a place of knowing it all. Far from it – we are all still on a journey, where the learning never ends. We are gifted with dark times and hard feelings for some purpose that we might not be able to see at the time, but that we can always learn from after the time.

Instead of the attachment that I felt to pain, I started to understand how that pain could help others. When things were hard I felt weak for asking for help and struggled, as so many of us do. But through coaching myself of the benefits to others, I allowed myself to break free from the need to hold everything in. I stopped judging how I was feeling and beating myself up for feeling bad. Be like a sieve, and allow your emotions and experience to pass through you. Speak out if something is troubling, to release the block and take a step towards living your happiest life.

— Day 9 —

OH WELL, DON'T DWELL

'Holding on to anger is like grasping a hot coal with the intent of throwing it at someone else; you are the one getting burned.'
THE BUDDHA

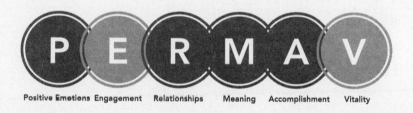

Positive Emotions Engagement Relationships Meaning Accomplishment Vitality

Did you know that much of the turmoil we experience is simply a mental illusion created in the mind? We all have an internal dialogue – sometimes referred to as the 'monkey mind' that chatters away in the background – working through past regrets, future worries and mental to-do lists, imagining worst-case scenarios for the future and projecting fears from deep within. Often, by the time we are ready to take action in the Now, we're already exhausted with all of the thinking we've done!

It can be particularly damaging to get caught up in reworking old memories of times when you feel you were wronged or to beat yourself up about something you should have done or not done. Getting out of victim mode requires an extra sense of awareness and a commitment to self-love, which we'll be working on later in this book. But the key to releasing yourself and moving forwards with peace lies in forgiveness – which is why both forgiveness of self and others is our focus today.

Forgiveness is a process that we intentionally undertake to change our feelings about someone we hold resentment and negative emotions towards, for something we feel has offended us or wronged us. Interestingly, this person is often ourselves. We tend to reserve forgiveness and the act of wishing someone well in relation to an indiscretion – such as a partner being unfaithful, or being bullied at school or by parents – for other people. However self-forgiveness and letting go of past mistakes and harmful thoughts is something that's vitally important to maintain and promote our psychological health.

The problem is that it's all too easy to cling on to negative feelings and resentments, and to keep going over and over the same old ground. Eventually, those harmful thoughts become so big and powerful that we wind up feeling worried and scared. I've been there. You've been there. Maybe you're there right Now. However, if you pause for a moment and recognize those hurtful thoughts as things you have powerfully created inside your mind being 'about you' rather than actually being you, you'll also realize that you have the power to let go of whatever is causing you hurt, whether that's someone else's judgement or perception, a past memory of regret or a mistake you made.

The power of forgiveness

Studies into the power of forgiveness show that forgiving does not mean forgetting, condoning, pardoning or excusing – and the goal of forgiveness is not always reconciliation.[1] Rather, forgiveness is something you do for yourself in order to reduce your level of psychological distress through the release of toxic negative emotions. It has been said that the opposite of love is not hate (rather, it's indifference), since hating someone takes just as much energy as loving them, with the direction of the energy being the only difference.

The negative energy and emotion that you put into holding on to anger and/or resentment can cause major negative health outcomes over time, while the other person suffers no further ill effects owing to unforgiveness. It seems that by not forgiving, you allow yourself to be victimized all over again and for an indefinite amount of time. Essentially, forgiveness allows you to take your power back. That said, forgiveness is something that you must freely choose and it's also something that will take some hard work.

That's true of self-forgiveness too, because when we're hurting or experiencing hard times, such as a messy break-up, stumbling over your words during a presentation or not speaking up during a meeting, any idea of self-love tends to be forgotten. This is because we mentally beat ourselves up for perceived or real mistakes, and allow our thoughts and emotions to spiral down and down. When you quiet the chatter of your monkey mind, and tame it through acceptance and forgiveness, then it becomes easier to let the past go and move on.

The fact is that life will continue to challenge us and at those times it can be hard to think clearly or act rationally, but the more you practise the art of self-forgiveness, the better you get.

#NOWISYOURCHANCE DAILY PRACTICE: FORGIVENESS AFFIRMATION

From today onwards, every time you find yourself beating yourself up, feeling resentment towards someone, having negative thoughts about yourself or lacking self-love, I'd like you to repeat one of the following affirmations for forgiveness – choose the one that feels true for you:

- 'I know that as I forgive others and myself, I expand into the next highest version of me.'

- 'Forgiveness allows me to access more joy and enables me to grow.'

- 'As I choose to let go of this negative feeling, I empower myself to move forwards with more strength and ease.'

You might also like to write your affirmations down. You might choose to fill an entire page in your notebook to really allow it to sink in, or write it down on a sticky note or card and carry it with you or place it where you'll see it often. Commit your self-forgiveness affirmation to memory and use it as often as you need, because the more you practise forgiveness, the more you'll show yourself the power of love.

###

Sometimes it's the events and experiences that really challenge us that help us to grow, because each one contains a valuable opportunity for us to learn something important. But in order to see the lesson, first we have to learn to forgive others and also forgive ourselves.

Using forgiveness to heal

I know that downloading the affirmation 'I forgive myself' into my consciousness became the healing tool I needed to move on and create a fresh start. While a messy break-up might not seem like a great Christmas gift, I knew I'd been clinging on to a codependent relationship for too long and it was time to move on. After three days of movies and tears, the realization came to me that I was torturing myself and that I simply needed to let go. The realization made me sit bolt upright and I began to write. Gratitude came tumbling out along with the tears and I started to work through forgiveness.

In that moment I felt a quantum shift and literally felt a dark cloud lift from me as I wrote down the words: 'I forgive myself for getting caught in a downwards spiral of negative thoughts and emotions, because the only person I'm hurting is myself,' over and over again. Done. I resolved to make a new plan and to do things a different way, on my own terms and armed with my new superpower of forgiveness.

I share this story with you with the intention that it will help you as powerfully as it helped me. Forgiveness creates an instant shift and allows us to let go. Use it when you need it and jump out of your downwards spiral. Like me, you might also find it helpful to play some uplifting music right after using this mantra. You can also use the following longer practice to help you find forgiveness and let go of any other resentment or thoughts that are holding you back from moving on:

#NOWISYOURCHANCE: LETTER OF FORGIVENESS

To help yourself in making this move, take 20 minutes today to write a letter of forgiveness to somebody you have been in conflict with or have shown resentment towards. This person might be someone from your past or somebody who is no longer in your life, or it might be appropriate to write this letter to yourself. How is holding on to this affecting you? How is it affecting the other person?

Now close your eyes and imagine as you begin to breathe deeply that you're breathing into that space where you previously held that memory or resentment.

Set the intention to release your pain, even if little bit by little bit. Imagine breathing in new, light energy and as you breathe out, imagine breathing out all of that pain and emotion you have held on to. See it floating away. Maybe you see it disappearing into the atmosphere, floating down a river or flying off high into the sky in light.

However you choose to visualize this, be sure to bless the person, yourself or the experience with love and forgiveness as you let go of the attachment to it. Remember: this is releasing you, not them.

###

The words 'I forgive...' really do allow us to let go of the pain we so easily direct towards ourselves, when we most need to show ourselves some love. So often we create a war for ourselves between our ears, and so often we choose to hold on to ill feelings and resentments, when in reality they only serve to stunt our growth. All experience is good experience, even if it doesn't feel like it at the time. The more we can learn to let emotion flow through us, and channel it for the highest good of others and ourselves, the more we can accept and move forwards from there.

Forgiveness an ongoing practice and can be the most difficult of all, but when we hold grudges or victimize ourselves, making others wrong, it's really an attack on our own wellbeing. By letting go of blame, we are able let go of the past, move into the Now and accept that sometimes it just is what it is.

— Day 10 —
MINDSET MAKEOVER

'The mind is its own place, and in itself can make a heaven of hell, a hell of heaven.'
JOHN MILTON, *PARADISE LOST*

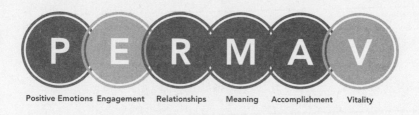

Positive Emotions Engagement   Relationships   Meaning   Accomplishment   Vitality

You know those days when you roll out of bed after hitting the snooze button five times, can't find your keys and your hair is a mess? We all have them. Well, it's not what happens to you that matters, but how you deal with it. Your mindset is a self-perception you hold about yourself, and it's also an asset that you can strengthen and grow. In PosPsych we talk about two types of mindset – fixed and growth.

A fixed mindset means seeing things as black and white – absolute success or absolute failure. If something goes wrong there's no getting away from it, and if someone challenges you… well, they had better watch out! The easiest way to notice if you're falling into a fixed mindset is to be aware when you start to get defensive or can feel resistance creeping in.

A growth mindset, however, supports happiness, growth and achievement because, in the words of Carol Dweck, the leading researcher in this field:

> *In a growth mindset, people believe that their most basic abilities can be developed through dedication and hard work—brains and talent are just the starting point. This view creates a love of learning and a resilience that is essential for great accomplishment.*[1]

A growth mindset focuses on the journey as well as the outcome. It also allows you to see challenge as a process to work through and an opportunity to serve your growth. You don't always need to be right. Instead you could pause and ask, 'Could I choose to see things a different way?'

You might notice whether you have a fixed or growth mindset when it comes to welcoming criticism, taking on challenges, thinking about your intelligence, making mistakes – and choosing to learn from them – because you know it serves your growth.

NIYC Notes

If you want to move from a fixed to a growth mindset, when you're feeling challenged ask, 'What can I learn from this?'

Mindset success

The research into mindset suggests that we all have both fixed and growth mindsets. A fixed mindset can often be triggered by a critical comment or not performing as well as peers, resulting in feeling insecure and defensive. But when we are self-aware, we can choose to shift into a growth mindset and use the challenge for personal growth. So instead of thinking of an athlete as 'talented', we would see that their success – and happiness – has been achieved through effort, consistency and practice. That's why some talented young people miss out on success, because they've been coached or taught to believe they are naturally gifted, and so fail to work on their mindset and put in as much effort to create the result.

The power of choosing to adopt a growth mindset was shown in two studies focusing on maths students in high school, in which practising a growth mindset proved to increase motivation and grades over two years. The students were found to have stronger learning goals and more positive beliefs about effort, and were less likely to demonstrate helplessness or give up.[2]

So when we put in the work and choose to adopt a growth mindset, the brain reorganizes and changes for the better, through a process called neuroplasticity, which is the brain's ability to reorganize itself by creating new neural pathways.

#NOWISYOURCHANCE DAILY PRACTICE: SHIFT YOUR MINDSET

When choosing to change the way you think, you're naturally required to take a new level of awareness. A great way to do this is to ask yourself questions. When you ask better questions, you get better answers. Start with the questions below, to help you gain a better understanding of where your mindset has been fixed in the past before, and how you can shift to take a new perspective and feel happier today.

Today, I'd like you to consider your answers to the following questions:

- Where can you notice that you have fallen into a fixed mindset before? (Remember: one of the big red flags is when you start to get defensive over something.)

- Where have you given up when things have become difficult?

- Where have you told yourself you're not 'intelligent' or 'talented' enough?

- Where have you made a mistake or failed at something and noticed yourself telling yourself you're no good?

- Where could you choose to take a growth approach to something that you're currently finding challenging?

- Where have you focused on making more effort in order to create results?

- Where can you consciously choose to accept criticism graciously, because you know it's helping you to learn?

- Where can you identify a challenge, struggle or something that feels hard for you and find gratitude for the process?

I used this self-inquiry exercise in a coaching program I ran for 4,500 entrepreneurs recently. When I asked for their reflections on what had been the most powerful element of the experience, it was their understanding and adopting of a growth mindset.

###

Consciously shifting mindsets

I know that if I don't remain conscious of my mindset then it leaves me feeling out of whack – like life isn't flowing properly – and, quite honestly, worn out and tired. This came home to me when I was on a retreat in Bali with my mastermind group. My coach was mapping out the process for shifting my coaching programme from being taught one-to-one to being taught as a blend of one-to-one and group sessions. I noticed some resistance to his words. After all, I'd helped so many clients to create amazing results with the one-to-one coaching model that I didn't see how changing it would be helpful. I could feel myself getting defensive and confused about how it would work.

However, I was also aware enough at this point to know that this was my fixed mindset slipping in. I was like a dog when their hackles go up and their hair stands on end. I took in the information and went outside for a walk during the break. I came back in refreshed and said to Ryan, 'I was feeling so much resistance there!'

'You're telling me!' he said!

But that's one of the big benefits of working with, and being surrounded by, other coaches and conscious people. It's that you know you'll always be called out if something comes up that's limiting your growth.

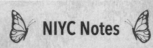

NIYC Notes

Think about all the different lotions and potions that you might have applied to yourself in the hope that they will make you look younger or more feminine or prettier. What if you dedicated the same time, care and attention to creating a growth mindset? Imagine investing that on your insides, your mental space, your You. What would be possible then?

It's not always easy to see our own behaviour and limits. Imagine that you're feeling wronged by someone or something, and you're spinning yourself a story about how unfair things are and how nothing is ever going to get any better. If you have a fixed mindset then you'll believe that and stay stuck there. Having a growth mindset, however, invites you to take a different approach. You're able to release yourself from negative feelings, where you've been telling yourself you're not good enough. Now armed with a growth mindset, you know that with effort, you can achieve all you desire. You're also able to reframe your experience, both from the past, within an instant and for the future, too. This means life becomes way more enjoyable and you'll love the journey so much more.

BE FIERCE!

'Expose yourself to your deepest fear;
after that, fear has no power.'
JIM MORRISON

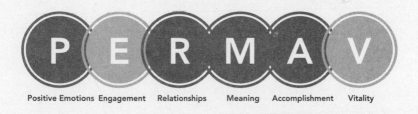

Positive Emotions Engagement   Relationships   Meaning   Accomplishment   Vitality

Would you give everything you've got to create everything you want? That's what it takes – a moment, a situation, an experience – when it comes to facing our fears. Big or small, today's challenge is to become aware of our fears, discover their root cause and overcome them. I know this may feel challenging, but as you know Now: if we don't step up to challenges, we can't grow. It can feel scary, but it doesn't have to be that way. So from Now on, whenever you face a fear, you'll know how to name it, claim it and move through it.

Understanding fear

We have around 60,000 thoughts per day – around 95 per cent of these are the same and up to 80 per cent can be negative![1] Over time these thoughts form into patterns of beliefs. The brain is programmed to protect us from potential harm and so responds more powerfully to negative stimuli such as danger, making it easier to soak up negative experiences and feelings.

What's more, it's really easy to stay feeling stuck, because the brain will always opt for what's familiar and safe over change. When it senses change, the brain produces fearful 'what if' thoughts that can keep us stuck in the wrong relationships, in bad habits and repetitive behaviour patterns, and in jobs that offer security when really we would love to start a business and travel. It can also impose psychological constraints on us that we might not even realize are there, until we start to look more closely.

Imagine your comfort zone with your beliefs about yourself and the world as the edge of that comfort zone. As you start to challenge those beliefs, you start to expand your experiences as you begin to question what you've always believed. For example, if you've been telling yourself for years that money is difficult to create, you'll continue to believe this and experience it within your reality. As you begin to challenge yourself, you'll gain a sense of accomplishment and start to feel better as you push out of your comfort zone, meaning that you're able to take on progressively bigger challenges each time.

A belief exists in the brain in a similar way to a memory: when it's repeated and the network of neurons fire again and again, the belief is strengthened. The amygdala is the part of the brain involved with recognizing threats and associated responses, and in forming beliefs. This is why when we become stressed, we are more likely to fall back on familiar patterns of behaviour. This means that old beliefs that have been strengthened over time are easy to revert to.[2] An example of this would be working on your mindset and experiencing success within your business then hitting a rocky patch. Your core beliefs are so strong that it's easy to allow the stressful experience to throw you off course, meaning you lose belief in yourself. This can be countered by repetition of a new powerful positive belief instead. As you break through a fear you step into your power, leave anxiety behind, and allow yourself to experience more joy and happiness.

Facing your fears

It's inevitable that we will all face situations and experiences that will test us. The trick is knowing what the fear is, so that we can deal with it, because fears are indicators that something magical is about to happen.

Once you have named your fear, it's time to claim it, own it and take responsibility for having created it from some part within you. Your fear is a projection of what might be, instead of what really is. You're being challenged to take fear by the proverbial horns, and flow with it and through it, instead of allowing it to stop you. As I described above, your brain loves you to stay where it feels familiar, so the challenge is to keep edging out of your comfort zone – or exploding out of there as is often the case! Choose not to be tricked into playing small or, even worse, giving up. You weren't created here to give up on yourself and your dreams weren't created for that purpose, either!

If it scares you, awesome!

#NOWISYOURCHANCE: OVERCOMING FEAR

To create a daily practice to overcome your fear, you need name it, claim it and choose to move through it. Use the following process daily or whenever you notice fear preventing you from moving forwards:

1. Take a moment to tune in to where in your life you feel stuck or desire a breakthrough.

2. Notice where you have prevented yourself from reaching towards a goal because you've told yourself it's impossible. It might be something big like changing careers or something smaller like going to a new gym class.

3. Then ask yourself what specifically you fear – is it the potential loss of income in the case of a career change, or feeling uncomfortable or uncoordinated in a new class. Get to the root of your fear by asking yourself what the belief is that's keeping yourself stuck. For example, 'I'll never be able to start a business because I don't have the money to invest,' or, 'I don't deserve to be treated well in a relationship because I wasn't treated well in my last relationship.'

4. Then ask yourself which part of this fear can you influence? For example, if you want to set up a business you might start by researching low-investment options, learning how to raise capital, or consulting with a mentor or coach.

5. Finally, consider which part you have no control over at all. For example, you can't change what happened in the past, so why allow the past to determine the future, when you have the power to change it?

Doing this exercise on a regular basis will help you to realize that you have way more control than you initially thought. Once you get clear on the fear, choose to take action towards the portion of the fear you can overcome by identifying the next positive step and then making a plan.

This might mean making and using a positive affirmation or defining the relationship that you want. And the part you're unable to control? Guess what? Let it go! The less time you spend worrying about and forcing the things you can't control, the more time you'll have available to allow your own exploration, intuition and intention to come through, so you can take action in the right direction!

#

 NIYC Notes

In his book *Tools of Titans*, Tim Ferris recounts an exercise he took part in at Tony Robbins' Unleash the Power Within event. I've practised this exercise with my coaches, and it involves examining your limited beliefs in the past, present and future – just like Scrooge was challenged to do so in Dickens' *A Christmas Carol*. The process takes at least 30 minutes and asks you to imagine how much your limited beliefs weigh on your life. With your eyes closed, you visualize the impact of your limited beliefs on your past, how they are affecting you Now in the present and what they are costing you for your future. You then choose three new positive beliefs and write them down, then imagine the trajectory of your life when you live with these affirmations every day. You'll notice a huge positive shift and experience much more happiness than before.

Facing off fear

I remember visiting my brother in New Zealand and feeling filled with fear. I'd left the UK a few months earlier in order to spend time writing and travelling, and coaching from my laptop along the way. Now my brother was telling me that I needed a job. I'd been running my business for a few years, but my savings weren't enough to support me for more than a few months. My newly launched online programme had seen a grand total of just one sign-up… and yet the prospect of a regular job made me feel sick to my core.

From that place of fear I applied for four jobs, each one feeling so completely out of alignment that I felt energetically drained and even more fearful that I was in the completely wrong place.

In actual fact, I was right where I was supposed to be, as we so often are, without realizing it at the time. The universe was asking me to step up and show her what I was made of, to get off the fence and move forwards towards what I wanted. That meant figuring out what was true for me.

In went my headphones, with back-to-back episodes of Marianne Williamson, Gabrielle Bernstein and Lewis Howes – all priming me for clarity and success. I knew that darkness comes before the dawn – hell, I'd been through enough darkness to last a lifetime and I knew that if I could get through that I could get through this!

I walked a loop for an hour a day, the same route, with a different podcast each time. I was soaking in as much positive learning as humanly possible and asking for guidance along the way. I meditated, as I always did, but this time with a new and powerful intention to help me find my way. I would pray and talk to the angels, and I knew that through by working on myself, the path becomes illuminated in front of me. I was intuitively guided towards Kundalini yoga, but when I scoured the Internet for a yoga class I was greeted with a big fat zero. No Kundalini in Wellington? WTF! Really? One of the most spiritually connected places I've been to and no Kundalini? Well, apparently the universe had other ideas for me that week and I was directed to a workshop with a clairvoyant named Jessica Reid, to make positive affirmations.

When I told my brother, Luke, about the class, he cried with laughter. 'What do you mean you sat on the floor and made bookmarks with glitter glue?' he asked, gasping for breath because he was laughing so much! 'Who else was there?'

I couldn't contain myself and I was laughing, too!

He and his fiancé, Hayley, do get me on some level, though, and they had kindly installed a noticeboard in my bedroom on which my new positive affirmations card held pride of place.

'I am fearlessly visible, and I boldly shine my light,' it read.

Over the next days and weeks I created a vision board, and filled it with goals, affirmations and positive focus to really help me shift from fear-based survival mode into what would ultimately become thrive mode, with a little (or a lot of) spiritual and business hustle in between.

I thought my fear had been one of my failures, but when I sat down to process it and name what was preventing me from going all in, I realized it wasn't a fear of failure, but rather a fear of being judged. I was scared of being seen! I flipped the negative thought of 'I'm scared of being judged' into 'I am fearlessly visible and I boldly shine my light.' I did this in the same way you might choose to take any fears that you've identified and flip them into the positive. So, for example, 'I am scared to quit my job in case my business fails' would become 'I boldly move forwards on my new path and trust that I am supported authentically in all that I choose to be and do.'

When I made the commitment to be fearlessly visible and got to work, I began to see that I needed to work differently, and things began to shift. Again I asked for guidance, this time through a meditation, and was gifted with a brand-new coach and mentor, who contacted me out of nowhere (thank you universe!), and gave me the confidence and the skills I needed to catapult into a whole new phase of growth.

#NOWISYOURCHANCE DAILY PRACTICE: CREATING A NEW REALITY

It's important to replace any limited beliefs that you've recognized with new empowering thoughts, feelings and intentions. For today's practice I want you to write out a new empowering affirmation and put it somewhere you can see it every day.

Make it look beautiful, whether that means creating a graphic and setting it as your desktop background or getting out your card, scissors and glitter glue, and making your own postcard, bookmark or key ring. If you have more than one affirmation you desire to work with, great!

Creating affirmations to overcome fears might not sound like much, but this simple action can instil a powerful fresh sense of self-belief that can help you to break through fears and limits, and change life for the better.

###

I've seen so many people quit before they've even got going, because fear stood in their way. Or rather, because they allowed fear to stand in their way. When you start to push at the edges of your comfort zone you'll be able to create massive and powerful change, by using your fear as fuel and finding the fire inside to help you thrive – but you have to choose it consciously.

You always have a choice in what you can accept as being the next determinant within your life. Is it fear that guides you and governs your choices, or is it your strength, your desires, your knowing, your intuition and your drive for something more?

MAKE CHOICES, NOT EXCUSES

*'I am not a product of my circumstances,
I am a product of my decisions.'*
STEPHEN COVEY

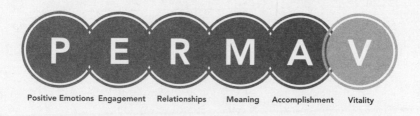

Positive Emotions   Engagement   Relationships   Meaning   Accomplishment   Vitality

Did you know that you are your own problem *and* your own solution? Learning and accepting this simple fact can help us to take responsibility for who we are, what we do, what we have and what we can create. It's important because so often it seems easier to pass the blame and make excuses for why things aren't going the way we want them to, but when you own yourself and your choices, you empower yourself.

I know I used to feel like I was having a rough ride, that my relationship wasn't working because the other person was doing things wrong, that my business wasn't working, despite trying so hard, or that I was feeling tired and I just didn't know why. But as soon as I started looking at myself and owning my thoughts and actions, I really began to understand how much of a part I had to play in all of this, too.

Decision-making

Successful entrepreneurs such as Richard Branson emphasize the importance of quick decision-making and even describe how it's often not the decision that matters, but making one and moving forwards.[1] That way you can quickly identify whether or not the decision was correct and adjust your actions accordingly. Now you're aware of the importance of maintaining a growth mindset (see Day 10, page 75), you may like to start to view all of your journey as a learning opportunity and understand that even though you may have made poor choices in the past, those choices allowed you to consciously make better choices in the Now and own your journey as you grow.

There are plenty of rational decision-making processes you can use, such as a SWOT analysis or writing lists of pros and cons. However, your decision-making processes are not always rational, and are instead privy to a whole host of emotional and subconscious biases, including your beliefs.[2] Instead of comparing options, we are likely to make a choice or decision based on how it makes us feel and how powerfully we can connect to the vision of the outcome in the future. What's interesting is that we know from the science of positive psychology that being in a positive mood and focusing on our strengths (see Day 7, page 49) allows us to be more creative, solution-focused, and to make decisions more effectively.[3-4]

Not making a decision is also something that's a choice and can keep us feeling stuck.

Instead of blaming and complaining, today is the day to take a long hard look at yourself and realize the true power of taking responsibility. Making excuses for the things not going to plan is an incredibly disempowering response. It leaves you feeling weak, victimized, like you don't know what to do next, and that you just want somebody to come along and pull you out of your shit. Well I have news for you – that person is always going to be YOU.

Build strength and personal power

When you spend time building your strength and personal power you can make choices that support your intended reality. If you start to take 100 per cent responsibility for every choice and decision you make, you'll start to see that you begin to make better choices. Instead of giving that power away and allowing yourself the backup of making an excuse for why you didn't do something or why something hasn't worked out exactly as planned, you're able to remind yourself that you made your choice and you can make another choice, and another. You can keep on going, choosing the next positive step and really owning your journey.

Designing your life only happens through choice and I've come across many people who actually keep themselves stuck in a reality they are not happy with, without even realizing they are doing it. For example, by:

- Comparing yourself to others.

- Procrastinating and missing out on opportunities.

- Not making a decision, and staying on the fence and in conflict.

- Staying in a routine or pattern of being that doesn't serve your vision of your highest self.

- Worrying about a decision you have made or have to make, without asking for help.

- Ignoring your gut feeling and intuition.

- Allowing fear of failure or embarrassment (or something else) to keep you from making progress.

All of the above serve as excuses for not creating our own happiness. We make excuses based on a whole host of things and can create this web of doing nothing but beating ourselves up. Whether the excuse is that you don't have enough time, the kids drove you to it or the dog ate it, none of them are going to stick here!

Now Is Your Chance to get clear about where you have been making excuses that are stopping you from stepping forwards into a reality that supports and nurtures the happiest version of you.

#NOWISYOURCHANCE: TAKE RESPONSIBILITY

In your journal, make a list of the biggest three excuses you're making for yourself right Now. For example, 'I'm always too busy,' 'I'm not making sales in my business because the quality of leads is so low,' 'I'm too old,' 'I'm too young,' 'I don't have enough time,' 'I can't be bothered,' etc.

Now, consider what choice you could make instead that would allow you to take a step in the right direction, heighten your experience of accomplishment, and live with more happiness and joy. For example, instead of complaining about being busy all of the time, choose to set aside an hour one evening to plan your week, commitments, priorities and where you can create space. List your choices in your journal, along with the commitment statement below:

'I am grateful to be creating my life consciously, based on the choices I make.'

###

Empowered action

When you begin drawing your attention to the areas where you can consciously choose to carve your own way, then suddenly the actions you need to take become clear. An empowered action is one that comes from a space of loving yourself so much that you can't possibly allow yourself to give that power away by making an excuse or externalizing blame. What I'm not suggesting is that you hate on yourself today. Quite the opposite, in fact!

Taking empowered action is a step forwards in building your personal resources. It allows you, step by step, to build strength of character and become the person who owns every choice and decision they make.

#NOWISYOURCHANCE DAILY PRACTICE:
MANTRA OF RESPONSIBILITY

Use the following mantra every day to support your thoughts and feelings with the intention of empowering yourself with self-responsibility.

'As I step up and claim responsibility for myself and my life I am able to move forwards with power and ease.'

Write it down, take it with you wherever you go and reflect on what feels true for you. What comes up for you when you write, speak or read the words, 'claim responsibility for myself'?

How does it feel to know that you always have the choice to do that?

###

— Day 13 —

KICK-ASS CONFIDENCE

*'I am the greatest. I said that
before I even knew I was.'*
MUHAMMAD ALI

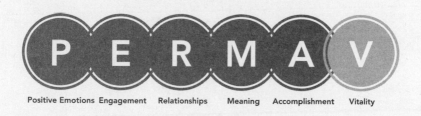

Positive Emotions Engagement Relationships Meaning Accomplishment Vitality

Where happiness and confidence grow, success and fulfilment flow, and while there is a lot to be said for lipstick and a good pair of heels, or a sharp suit and a clean shave, to kick-start your day, we ultimately need to stop comparing our insides to other people's outsides. It's easy to create an ideal view of somebody else's happiness or success, when you're looking at what they want you to see. The difference being that you don't know how another person feels – only what they choose to have you believe.

When coaching women from around the world, (many of whom are inspirational leaders, high-powered executives, and successful entrepreneurs with six-figure, seven-figure, eight-figure and even nine-figure businesses), I notice again and again that they struggle with self-doubt. Self-doubt seems to be something that transcends sex, geography and profession, and at every step of your journey, success or the pay scale, a new challenge presents itself that allows self-doubt to creep back in.

The role of self-esteem

Inspirational leader and speaker John Maxwell suggests that self-esteem is the single most significant key to a person's behaviour. He also goes on to say:

> If your desire is a 10 but your self-esteem is a 5, you'll never perform at the level of a 10. You'll perform as a 5 or lower. People are never able to outperform their self-image.[1]

This is why today's task is to work on your self-image, boost your self-esteem, and to make a commitment to continue this work on yourself each and every day.

You already know that physical activity is one way to boost the way you feel about yourself (see Day 4, page 27) and that the confidence extends outwards as a ripple effect into other areas of your life – but what else do we know from the science of happiness about confidence and positive self-image?

Self-esteem is known to correlate with positive life satisfaction and skills, and negatively correlate with aggression, depression, poor performance, alcohol and drug abuse, and marital dysfunction, amongst others.[2] It's widely accepted that self-esteem has a strong relationship with happiness,[3] and self-efficacy theory – as outlined by prominent psychologist Albert Bandura[4] – is actually fundamental to the field of PosPsych.

Self-efficacy is the belief in your own ability to influence and control events that affect your life and how they are experienced. We all have it, and we are all able to strengthen it, as Bandura suggests, through practice and mastery, the finding of role models and effective mentors, and by creating a peak state with positive emotions. With this knowledge and empowered standpoint, I hope you can see the importance of working on your confidence here today.

Much like fear, self-doubt is significant in that it allows you to notice where you're being gifted with an opportunity to grow. It's natural that we question ourselves – and self-doubt, in fact, provides an opening for reflection. It gives us the opportunity to examine our goals and choices, and decide if we really want to keep travelling in that direction.

For example, you might experience self-doubt in relation to your career and think, 'Can I really achieve this success?' or, 'Am I really good enough to get this next promotion?'

Of course you can and of course you are!! Fear will naturally come up from time to time and each phase of your growth will require an increase in self-belief. Self-doubt might creep in when you wonder if you're good enough to get that guy you've had your eye on for a little while, or if it's possible to launch your blog and not look like an idiot. The fact is the difference between where you are now and where you want to be always boils down to one of two things:

- a skills gap; or

- a mindset gap

Most of the time it's the latter. Self-doubt might try to trick you into thinking that you need to be something other than yourself, by trying to convince you that you need to be better at something new. More often than not, what you need to get better at is being you.

There are a few things that can stunt our ability to build our confidence and grow our self-belief, so let's look at each one in turn:

Comparing yourself to other people

There is so much comparison in our world. Social media platforms like Facebook are fantastic for increasing engagement and positive emotions, and allowing emotional expression – which in turn increases connection and confidence – but they can also open up the opportunity for one-upmanship, and the tendency to look at other people's lives and compare them with our own. It's awesome to have role models and create more inspiration and motivation, but when you're slamming yourself on the inside and trying to keep up with others on the outside, you really are making things so much harder than they need to be.

Use comparison and competition to fuel you, not diminish you, and look to learn from those you admire instead of letting the comparison get you down.

NIYC Notes

If browsing on social media is doing you more harm than good, then try taking a social media detox for a few days or weeks and see how you feel. I have friends who have tried this with fantastic results!

Listening to negative people around you

Not everyone has the awareness, intention and willingness that you do when it comes to keeping a positive perspective. That's life. Quite often, those around you will not understand you, what you do and why you do it. Newsflash for you – they don't need to!

When trying to get a message across, we don't always communicate in the most effective ways. It can be easy for our words to be misconstrued if we are feeling sensitive or not at our best, or unsure of how to say what we mean to say and the impact that it might have. I encourage you to maintain a growth mindset (see page 76), as this will stand you in good stead when allowing comments to flow over you instead of affect you.

A negative comment or lack of support from somebody else says more about them than it does about you. When someone dents your confidence – when you choose to allow someone to dent your confidence – it's important that you do something to build it back up. Immediately. Remind yourself that your map of the world isn't everybody else's map of the world and that (in the words of Marianne Williamson) 'all acts of communication are either an act of love or a cry for help'. When you check in with this truth, it allows you to let go of the attachment to other people's words. You can then replace their words with something more positive in your mindset. Instead of wallowing in self-pity or questioning your ability based on what someone else thinks or says, put in place a positive replacement that reminds you of the good things you are and do.

I know that it used to get me down that my dad didn't understand or support my work and that he always wanted me to get a job. He could see that I'd spent five years at university and had worked so hard, but that I had very little to show for it. I loved my business but I was busy, exhausted and struggling. Because he couldn't feel or see my vision, he thought that the solution was to quit. Giving up has never been an option for me though, and even in the face of my dad and so many others thinking I was crazy for doing what I do, I kept going… and I'm glad I did.

Your own negative self-talk

The way you speak to yourself has a profound impact on how you feel. When you're putting yourself down or self-depreciating, you're likely to be lowering your self-confidence, too. Imagine going in to a job interview having incanted to yourself, 'I can't do this, this isn't the job for me, I am terrible compared to the other candidates and I'm never going to get this.' Much more than defensive pessimism, this negative thinking will take you down faster than anything else. It's going to leave you feeling bad about yourself, you'll be less than happy and you'll find it harder to pluck up the courage to have another go. This is why it's essential to commit to improving your self-talk, and keeping your beliefs, thoughts, actions, words and perspective in the positive.

 NIYC Notes

Use the following kick-ass affirmation to help supercharge your confidence:

'I am grounded, peaceful and content, and I accept myself fully. I am always more than good enough.'

Doing the work

Choosing just to do nothing is a no-no. We have one life to feel and be our best, and we might as well start Now. Self-mastery starts but never ends. Our work on ourselves is never done, because we are always constantly growing and evolving. Our environments are changing, and we are challenged with new experiences and interactions. If you don't work on yourself you'll get left behind.

Confidence is developed by first acknowledging that you would love to have some more of it. Once you know what you want, you can go and get it. Here follows five of my tried-and-tested methods to build your self-esteem:

1. Reflect on times you have felt confident, accomplished and proud

By connecting back to times that you have felt confident and believed in yourself, you're proving that it's possible to have felt that way before and so it's possible to feel that way again. You might recall a time when you felt confident speaking in front of other people, or when you said something you were fearful of saying, or when you rocked that LBD and felt a million dollars. You now have actual evidence that you're awesome.

2. Let go of social comparison

Choose one situation of judgement or social comparison that you can let go of today. For example, you might choose to let go of comparing yourself to that friend who always seems to have everything in check.

Complete this affirmation in relation to the situation that you're choosing to let go of:

'Every day, in every way, I am getting better and better at _____.'

For example, you might say, 'Every day, in every way, I am getting better and better at being myself, loving myself and knowing that my best is always good enough,' or 'Every day, in every way, I am getting better and better at owning my worth and letting go of self-comparison.'

3. Identify your cheerleaders

Who in your world is always there to support you? Who builds you up instead of putting you down? Who helps you to stand tall and proud as you are? Write a list of these people, and choose to spend more time talking to and being with them. Aim to be this person for other people, too.

4, Practise self-care

Giving yourself a little time and space can do wonders for your self-worth. By choosing to give to yourself instead of push yourself all of the time, you send a subtle signal that you're worth it. You're worth the space, or the kind words, or the flowers. The little moments of joy will help you to boost your confidence.

5. Get out of your comfort zone

As we explored on Day 11 (see page 81), there's nothing quite like challenging yourself to really help you grow! When you stretch yourself, you build your confidence. Start with something small that you know will challenge you but that's still possible and allow your confidence to grow bit by bit. For example, you might choose to attend a gym class with a friend before going along on your own. Or you might choose to practise smiling and making proper eye contact with your close friends and family before you practise it with strangers, too.

You might also like to make a bucket list of all of the big things you'd love to do but have been putting off. Maybe it's a sky dive, or visiting a new destination, or going out to dinner alone. Choose one of these things and take a bold stand for your own self-confidence, by making a plan to do one of these big things within the next few months. It feels fantastic to know you have overcome something big and means all of your little challenges start to pale in comparison.

#NOWISYOURCHANCE DAILY PRACTICE: SUPERCHARGE YOUR SELF-ESTEEM

Choose (at least) one item from the list of self-belief boosting strategies listed earlier. Put this into practice in your life today.

###

Dedicating time, intention and attention to your self-confidence, self-worth and how you feel is an investment that will always pay dividends. When you build your self-belief, you're much better equipped to deal with challenges that come your way as you continue to grow. I'm not promising there won't be difficult things to navigate in the future. But when you do the work from today's teachings, you'll find that you greet and cope with challenges more quickly and easily than before.

— Day 14 —
GEEK IS CHIC

'Happiness is not to be found in knowledge,
but in the acquisition of knowledge.'
EDGAR ALLAN POE

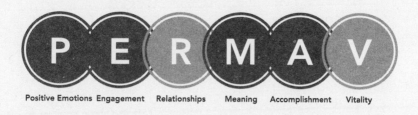

Positive Emotions Engagement Relationships Meaning Accomplishment Vitality

We've been looking at how each concept within this book links back to the PERMA-V theory, of which engagement is an integral part. Learning something new is a fantastic way to increase our level of engagement and when we experience engagement, we start to flourish. The commitment to mastery and learning helps to build self-efficacy and is actually a core need for psychological wellbeing, too – you build your mental capacity and resources through education.

Now by learning, I don't just mean study – life is not a textbook. By learning I mean soaking up as much as possible from the rich and vast teachings that life offers us. Our world is abundant and with so much available to us, you might think we would take the universe up on her offer of helping us expand and grow. So don't think learning has to involve textbooks or exams, as your learning might mean taking another course or learning a new skill. Similarly, it might be a conversation, an appreciation, a feeling or a nuance you can pick up on.

Being immersed in learning can also induce a state of flow, where time passes unnoticed, in which you're highly focused and have a huge sense of satisfaction after completion. This is because you have been so focused in the Now.[1] People who continue to learn throughout their lives have also been found to live longer and get better jobs. They are also healthier and less stressed.

Nerding out

There was a time when nerding out wasn't so cool, but now geek is so chic. Whether it's a pair of Chanel glasses, a NASA space pen (yes, I have one!) or the latest piece of software that you're going fan-girl crazy for... working on yourself and investing in yourself is so hot right Now. As you open up your heart and mind to really start to see the infinite possibilities that surround you and lie within you, you can begin to grasp just how much capacity you have to transform your life.

One by one by one, if we all commit to doing the work on and for ourselves, the ripple effect extends outwards, creating a bigger shift. A love of learning is one of the character strengths that we all hold within us and one that can be nurtured to help us thrive. Once you learn something, you have that knowledge, that wisdom, for life and nobody can take that away. Think about your learning as if it were a toolkit (which it absolutely is), beginning with the basic pack – the essentials that you acquire through childhood to help you grow. Then you add some higher-order skills and your mental toolkit gets bigger. Each time you learn something, you expand into a higher version of yourself as you add to your emotional, spiritual and practical resources. Soon you have the bonus pack, which you carry everywhere with you, meaning that you're equipped for life, wherever you go.

One of my friends who asks a lot of questions inspired today's daily practice. Whether he's at dinner or in the store or with friends, he always takes the time to ask questions and listen to the answers he's given. Through this simple act he has researched and amassed an understanding of a whole host of things simply by being curious. The tendency might be to keep your head down, your eyes on your phone and pass the checkout girl with little more than a robotic, 'Hello'. But what if you started to ask questions? What else might be possible then?

Ask more questions today, my love, for they will bring you more answers.

#NOWISYOURCHANCE DAILY PRACTICE: ASK MORE QUESTIONS

Today's practice is about adding to your mental and spiritual resources by seeking to explore more, to learn about our world, yourself and other people. It's really easy too, particularly when you take a more mindful approach to life (see Day 23, page 171).

Simply be aware of where can you pause in the Now and ask a question that allows you to learn something new.

You might also like to think about what topics you would love to learn about. Maybe you're really interested in finding out more about Brazil, but you've never really got round to it. Or maybe psychology is more your thing. Answer the following questions and note down any observations in your journal:

- Where can you learn from today? (This might mean picking up a book on a topic you haven't yet explored or you might choose to listen to a new podcast instead.)

- Who can you learn from today? (This might be one of your grandparents, a child, one of your role models, a friend or someone in business.)

- What questions can you ask?

Consider what open questions will give you the most interesting, powerful and insightful answers – and expect to be surprised!

###

Get curious

Approaching life with a childlike curiosity can afford us so much more of an adventure within our journey. To think we have it all figured out is to fail to see from another perspective, which can lead to getting stuck. When you understand there is always room for growth and you say, 'Thank you' and 'What else is possible now?' you open up both your consciousness and your willingness to allow more greatness to flow in.

Imagine 100 years ago trying to explain to somebody that they could fly to another continent in a matter of hours, eat gourmet food and sleep in a bed on board – they would think you had lost your mind! Advancements in technology such as the aeroplane, the iPhone and the electric car would not have been possible without the burning craving for more knowledge, more understanding and vision.

#NOWISYOURCHANCE: INNOCENT AWARENESS

Use this practice to help bring your younger, more curious self to each and every day, helping you set the intention to learn something new.

Before using this practice for the first time, you might like to spend a little time thinking about what it means to be a kid playing in the garden. For example, I watched as my friend's nieces chased a dandelion flower in awe and amazement as it floated in the wind. Next, a cat mesmerized them. Imagine what your day would look like if you approached it with more childlike curiosity and interest in everything! We would probably be a tiny bit less productive and a whole lot more happy. Sometimes I feel like a kid when I feel so much awe and wonder in even the tiniest thing. Now it's your turn:

1. Close your eyes and take a few deep breaths. As you breathe and start to relax, bring to mind a memory of when you were younger and you felt really happy. Maybe a time when you were five or six years old.

2. Feel what it feels like to be little again, without a care in the world. You felt so happy and carefree. Feel the feeling of

freedom, of joy, as you laugh and smile and play. Stay here for a moment, and feel that freedom and that joy. Your younger self is so happy and joyful!

3. Hear the sound of you laughing as your younger self! Make that sound out loud Now!

4. Feel your innocent awareness as you play and laugh, and your curiosity as you take in your world around you. WOW!

Take a few more deep breaths and allow the feeling to build and expand inside of you as you open your eyes.

###

— Day 15 —

ABRACADABRA!

'Language creates reality. Words have power. Speak always to create joy.'
DEEPAK CHOPRA

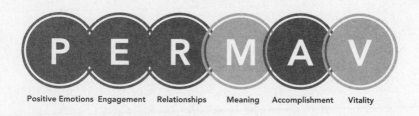

Positive Emotions Engagement Relationships Meaning Accomplishment Vitality

Did you know that the thoughts you think and the words you speak have the power to bring new life into your reality? Be it good or bad, the things we say have power. The word 'abracadabra' literally means, 'I create as I speak'. With this in mind, when we are navigating our days with the intention of being happy, it's important that our narration supports that.

How can you create a life of joy, if you're telling yourself (and other people, too) that you're tired, you feel fat and your partner is driving you crazy? When you're spending too much time focused on what's wrong, how on earth can you find the space for what's right?

Paying attention to your language and the words you use can really help you to shift more of your energy onto those things and thoughts that support your happiest and best life. And it starts by listening in to yourself.

The Law of Attraction

How many times a day do you hear yourself saying, 'I can't', or 'I'm so stupid' or 'I'm tired'? The law of attraction states that you can conceive and create anything you desire in your life once you get on the matching vibration to that thing you want, but it can also mean that you can attract more of what you don't want by focusing on it.

From Now on, I'd like you to imagine your life as a series of possibilities, where you have a choice which reality you choose. You're browsing an imaginary brochure in your mind, and you make your selection based on what you desire, what you believe you deserve and what you consistently think about.

You might be tempted to dismiss this idea, but the law of attraction is grounded in science, as it has been proven that being positive and optimistic leads to better health and relationships and faster progress towards your goals. It also helps you live longer (there's an entire chapter coming up on this later in the book). The discovery of mirror neurons shows us that our brain is activated to replicate an emotion or action when seeing it in somebody else.[1] The premotor and parietal cortex are activated when you observe movement, and the amygdala is activated when you observe emotions such as fear and happiness, which your brain then replicates. This means when you radiate smiles and exude awesome, others around you will mirror that, too. What you focus on grows, so make sure you're focusing on, and speaking of, what it is you desire.

It works on a subtler plane, too. Saying to yourself, 'I have to do this work,' or 'I have to go meet this friend,' suggests struggle, obligation and conflict. It also suggests that you're doing something you don't want to do. But change these words to, 'I love to do this work,' or 'I'm excited to meet with this friend,' and you change your reality to suit.

#NOWISYOURCHANCE: SPEAK HAPPY

To cultivate more positive language and attract more good into your life, I'd like you to reflect on a conversation you've had recently and determine your level of positivity. Answer the following questions in your notebook, and use your writing and journaling to support your development of a positive vocabulary:

- What words did you use?

- What meaning do these words have?

- How might I say things differently next time?

- Then, with your answers to the questions in your mind, be intentional about the conversations you have with people for the rest of your day.

###

Choosing your words

Minding your words matters when talking with other people and about other people, too. You never know how someone else might interpret your words and so how you communicate really matters. You might make a fleeting comment in jest about the way somebody looks or behaves, not meaning to hurt their feelings. But if that comment comes across as cutting to the person receiving it, it will impact them in a negative way. If you knew how much harm a negative could create years down the line, would you pause and think a moment longer before you spoke? I suggest you do.

Similarly, you never know how your words might impact somebody else positively and an encouraging word or reflection on somebody's character might just be the thing that picks that person up when they need it most. I remember my friends' Steff and Jess' mum saying to me, 'Nicola, you're brilliant. You are, you're brilliant,' and that has stayed with me to this day. Hearing those words from somebody I respected gave me confidence in myself and made me work even harder towards my goals, with the reinforced belief that I had what it took to make it work. Something that means nothing to you might stand out for somebody else – be it in a good way or in a bad way.

Words create feeling and meaning, and can last a lifetime or longer. Do you want to be remembered for speaking positively or be referred to as the person who was always bitching and gossiping? When you focus on making happiness your way of life, you find you don't have time for gossip and instead get on with the potential you have for making things good.

#NOWISYOURCHANCE DAILY PRACTICE: GET MINDFUL OF YOUR TRIGGERS

I'm challenging you to get mindful of the triggers that send you into a negative swirl. Perhaps you have a friend who always moans and complains, so when you're together you do it, too? Maybe it's when something goes 'wrong' you forget your power and sink into blame and complain mode. Or maybe it's the morning times when you need a little bit of extra get up and go that you notice your negative voice comes through. Whatever it is for you, I encourage you to be mindful today and expand your awareness, so you notice these danger zones and can stop them in their tracks.

###

When my coach asked me who I looked up to as a role model and who inspired me to be better, I reflected a little and came up with this: 'My friend Nick who lives in LA. Like me, he's from Newcastle and is hugely successful – he sold his first online business when he was in his teens and is now a successful company director. One of the many things I really admire about him is that he is really humble and doesn't speak badly about people. He always has something good to say.'

When you always have something good to say, you're remembered for that. Would you rather be spoken about favourably in this way like Nick, or be known as the person who seems to hate the world and everything in it?

The power of positive speech

The words you choose to speak can also prove powerful in creating new feelings and beliefs. When working on your goals and vision for your happiest life (which we'll be doing soon), saying what you want to create out loud can help you to make it so. In his documentary movie *I Am Not Your Guru*, Tony Robbins shares how he created his feeling of power from within by repeating to himself out loud over and over again, 'I am unstoppable.'

Reinforcing the positive like this and speaking what you desire to create is vital in helping you shift into a positive space instead of slipping into a downwards spiral of pain. Your first step before you even get to this point is to quiet the negative, and stop blaming and complaining.

#NOWISYOURCHANCE:
SAVE THE BLAME, DON'T COMPLAIN

Challenge yourself to one day of no complaining! That's right – an entire day without a moan or a whinge or a negative word. You'll quickly become aware of how much you were complaining and blaming beforehand, and this mindfulness will help you to see what's possible when you speak in the positive.

###

Day 15: Abracadabra!

As you shift your thoughts and words more into the positive, you'll naturally experience more positive feeling as a result. You'll no longer be a spectator in your life, but rather an active and engaged participant, who has fun consciously creating through the spoken word. Your relationships will improve and you'll have a sense of satisfaction for having created a certain level of mastery.

— Day 16 —

MORE THAN JUST SKIN DEEP

*'A smile is a window to the
beauty found within.'*
Dr Esho

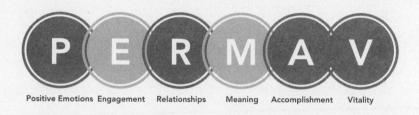

Positive Emotions Engagement Relationships Meaning Accomplishment Vitality

When I asked my mum what she was wearing to dinner one evening, she replied, 'A smile!' – and what a beautiful thing to be wearing, too. It's easy to think that happiness is found in wearing a designer dress, carrying the latest handbag, or having your eyebrow and lip game on point. But at the end of the day, when all of this is dropped, what do you really have that makes you happy? It's a trick question really, because it's not always what we have, but in fact what we choose to be and focus on that brings us greater and deeper happiness.

Consider the new wave of harsh self-comparison that has arisen via the popularization of celebrity magazines, photo-editing apps and the cosmetic surgery craze – first we saw size 0 happen, then came the Kim K bum, and now it seems that every blogger has their own fashion line, Ferrari and flawless body that just leaves you wanting more.

When you hate on yourself, you wind up playing a game of emotional snakes and ladders – one day you're high as a kite, loving life, and the next minute you're hung up on someone's most recent Instagram photo, at which point your inner world comes crashing down inside you. The intention is to even out the conflict we create for ourselves within, to allow for more self-love and more building each other up instead of tearing each other down.

What's in a smile?

We know from research that smiling is great for your wellbeing – one smile releases the same amount of endorphins as 2,000 bars of chocolate! You're also thought to be more trustworthy when you smile genuinely to someone. This kind of smile is known as a 'Duchenne smile', named after the 19th-century French physician Dr Guillaume Duchenne, and can be identified when your eyes crinkle at the corners. It's thought that when your smile involves the orbicularis oculi muscles at the top of the cheeks and around the eye, you're experiencing an authentic moment of joy.[1] I just got the warm and fuzzies, did you? What's more is that if you're faking a smile, you still benefit from results like increased energy, lowered stress and an ability to see less of what's wrong and more of what's right with the world.[2]

Instead of choosing to feel less than (because by now you understand that, just like happiness, self-depreciation is a choice you make), understand that happiness comes from being happy in your own skin, being self-aware and getting to know who you are. Stop comparing what you feel on the inside to what you see on other people's outsides, and instead start seeing inspiration and motivation rather than an opportunity to self-hate.

#NOWISYOURCHANCE DAILY PRACTICE: SELF-LOVE MANTRA

Whenever you notice yourself being self-critical, pause and smile, and then repeat the following affirmation:

'As I accept myself and love myself I allow my own happiness to grow.'

###

Creating self-worth through love

Sending yourself love helps to boost your positive emotions, confidence and self-worth. A smile is always going to look so good on you, and it allows you to radiate your inner bliss and beauty when you genuinely let it shine. I challenge you to remember the last time someone's resting bitch face caught your eye, you listened to them moan about how awful the world is and then you exclaimed to yourself, 'OMG, this person is so beautiful right Now!'

We are so much more likely to see beauty in someone who is smiling, with that twinkle in their eye that suggests they are within a joyful moment. That smile and joy radiates outwards and creates a ripple effect, and will always be worth so much more than the skin-deep pleasures found in more cosmetic pursuits.

Direct your attention and intention towards the little steps in positive thought and experience that you can take to support yourself with more self-compassion and less self-judgement. Remember to look for both the good in you and the good in others, and be the person who gives a smile first today – it costs absolutely nothing and can make somebody's day.

#NOWISYOURCHANCE: AWESOME THINGS ABOUT ME

Use the following questions to celebrate all that you are. Work through each section in turn, making sure you write at least three things for each section:

- Which three positive words can you use to describe you? For example, tenacious, intrepid, unstoppable.

- What do you love about your body? For example, I love my eyes that allow me to see, I love my legs that carry me through each day and I love my lungs that help me to breathe without even thinking about it.

- What do you love about your personality? For example, I am kind, I am funny and I am forgiving.

- What do you love about your mind or abilities? For example, I love that I always see the good in people, I love that I am great at reframing a difficult situation to create a new opportunity and I love my ability to get stronger as things get harder.

- Now ask the same four questions to somebody else to hear all of the good things about you, from their point of view.

###

— Day 17 —

WHY?

*'Don't ask yourself what the world needs;
ask yourself what makes you come alive,
then go do that. Because what the world
needs is people who have come alive.'*
HOWARD THURMAN

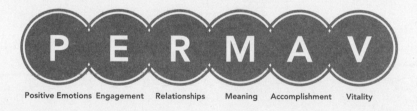

Positive Emotions Engagement   Relationships   Meaning   Accomplishment   Vitality

Leading a talk in Hollywood about how to create the best version of you, I asked the audience to pick out which of the five key elements for thriving they felt that they were missing the most.

For one audience member that question created a flash of illumination and he shared that he was missing meaning in his life. He partied, worked and was writing a screenplay, but he didn't really know why. That bigger purpose and 'why' was missing for him, and this is something that I notice again and again.

One of the key components of living a happy and thriving life is to find meaning and purpose – it's the 'M' in the PERMA-V theory. It's researched in depth within the science of positive psychology, where meaning is positively related to hope and fulfilment, and is considered as being made up of four distinct components that make up the PURE model:[1]

- Purpose

- Understanding

- Responsible action

- Enjoyment/evaluation

Your experience of positive emotions will broaden and build your psychological resources, and make you more resilient when times get tough and you find yourself soul searching. Having a sense of meaning is what will get you through.

 NIYC Notes

A Man's Search for Meaning by holocaust survivor Victor Frankl is one of the texts recommended to us as positive psychologists learning about meaning. It tells the story of a Nazi concentration camp survivor who found purpose and meaning even in the most desperate of times.

Your big 'why' might be to find happiness for yourself and your family, or to find freedom, or create something in the world that's bigger than you. When you connect in with your why, you really find your power.

I'm blessed to have found my calling at an early age. At 18, I gave up my scholarship to study mechanical and automotive engineering at university, after a conversation with my partner, Nicky, who was a professional cricket player at that time.

We were living out in Australia and he came back to our hotel room with a story about the session he had just had with his sports psychologist. He led him through a visualization of standing out on the cricket pitch when in to bat, and choosing not to look at the fielders around him, but to focus on the gaps in between the fielders instead. This struck a chord with me, as I realized, in life, we must focus not on the obstacles we see around us, but on the opportunities instead. That breakthrough was enough to shift my mindset, connect with my purpose, and change my degree path from engineering to sport and psychology.

My purpose became to help people, and over the years my purpose has grown and become more specific. My big mission is to help at least a million people change their lives using positive psychology, and to donate at least $1million to charity to help survivors of domestic violence, rape and human trafficking. For me, the mission is so much bigger than me, and I know that through my work I can create so much more for you and humanity. As I grow, my influence and potential to impact more people more powerfully grow, too. I know that through growing my brand and my business, I can reinvest in projects that help to make my mission a reality, and then help that mission to grow further and expand again, too. I can also help my family and mobilize additional vehicles to put the tools in the hands of the people who need them most.

Change might be created in a minute or in a month and when that moment comes, and a client comes back to me and says, 'You've changed my life, Niyc,' it always makes me smile. I find so much joy in knowing that they altered the course of their life, and allowed themself to feel better more of the time. I will always tell them: 'I didn't change your life, you did.' I just help clients see the steps, then they can empower themselves to take the action.

So what's your why?

If you feel like you're kind of floating or coasting through life right Now, and you're lacking that purpose that allows your goals and desires to become meaningful for you, start to consider what it is that's really important to you. What are you passionate about and what really brings you joy? Is there a cause or an issue that's important to you? Are you working for the good of your children and your family? Do you find motivation to get through the day by knowing that you're simply serving the highest good of others and yourself? What is it that makes you come alive?

A happy life is a fulfilled life, and the intention is that you find fulfilment through living on purpose and experiencing and creating the things you enjoy and find meaning in.

#NOWISYOURCHANCE: UNDERSTANDING YOUR WHY

Today is all about finding out your big WHY and connecting in with it to allow you the sense of knowing that your actions are on purpose. Answer the following questions to determine your why:

- What brings you joy and makes you feel alive?

- What things motivate you into action?

- Who is important to you?

- What problem do you hate to see in the world?

- What value do you create/desire to create for others?

- What's your unique strength/ability/brilliance?

- What's your mission and your big why?

###

#NOWISYOURCHANCE DAILY PRACTICE: SUPPORT YOUR GOALS

Now you have got clear on your mission statement and why reason, let's look at how you can use it to support your goals. I want you to set a goal for 12 months in the future, and work backwards to identify where you would like to be on your journey towards this goal in three, six and nine months' time. These quarterly goals will help you to stay on track and they provide the perfect timeframe to allow you to make a burst of effort, without getting burned out. So take out your journal and jot down the following:

- My 12-month goal is...

- My nine-month goal is...

- My six-month goal is...

- My three-month goal is...

Now, consider what you need to do and who you need to be on a monthly, weekly and daily basis in order to achieve these goals. Do you need to be more consistent? Do you need to commit to listening to something positive and motivational every day to remind you of your why and keep you making progress?

- The things I need to do each month are...

- The things I need to do each week are...

- The things I need to do daily are...

- Who I need to be to fulfil my purposeful goals is...

- How I will remind myself of my big why reason daily is...

When you connect with your passion, get clear on your purpose and link your goals with your why, there is no stopping you. You're happy, more aligned and engaged with the activities and work you do in your life.

###

— Day 18 —

SEE THE GOOD IN EVERYTHING

'Optimism is a happiness magnet. If you stay positive, good things and good people will be drawn to you.'
MARY LOU RETTON

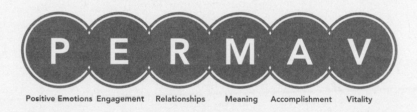

Positive Emotions Engagement Relationships Meaning Accomplishment Vitality

I really don't see the point of being negative when we can choose to be positive and find a solution. I always like to feel happy and when I am able to make a choice that supports my happiness, I'm damn well going to choose it. Today, I'll show you how you can, too.

By no means am I suggesting that you ignore emotions that are indicative of feeling and releasing pain – I did that for a looong time and it came back to bite me. What I am suggesting is that through daily hassles you find the awareness to divert your attention to what's positive and possible. During hard times, allow your emotion to flow, while understanding there is both a silver lining and always a light at the end of the tunnel.

Attaching to hope and a positive outcome can give your spirit strength, and allow you to keep on going when times feel tough. Remind yourself of your growth mindset (see Day 10, page 75) and choose the perspective here that all experience offers some sort of learning, opportunity or growth. If you don't see it right Now, it will be on its way to you. The activity at the end of this chapter will help you.

Up to this point you have survived 100 per cent of your days and the opportunity Now is to build on that survivor within you, so you can grow and thrive. You've stepped out of victim mode and decided to stop just surviving. Now, you're stepping up to flourish and thrive – with a whole new world at your fingertips should you decide to choose it.

#NOWISYOURCHANCE: SPOT THE POSITIVE

When you look back on your past year, notice the opportunities that allowed you to find happiness in an instant. Also notice where you may have sometimes constricted the energy and opportunity by stopping the positive flow and worrying about or becoming fixated on what's going wrong. Take a note of the following in your journal:

- A place I focused on happiness was…

- A place I blocked my own happiness was...

- A place I can start choosing to see the good in everything is...

###

The benefits of optimism and hope

An optimistic approach has been shown in studies to lead to having better physical and psychological health, to allow for the experience of more positive relationships and emotions, to increase the chances of success and to help you reach your goals more quickly. When you believe in the possibility of an outcome, you're more likely to work hard towards it.[1] Optimism activates the rostral anterior cingulated cortex (RACC) and the amygdala in the brain, to help us draw upon emotions from memories of events, and also downplay any negative experiences or predictions. Optimism allows us to appraise situations in a more positive light, thus preventing lasting down ticks in our emotional response – basically, you freak out less! Optimists are less stressed, more resilient and will live longer, too!

There can be a downside to optimism, however, and through seeing the good in everything and every person, and by being the YES! person who is enthusiastic about plans and ideas, can mean underestimating the time it takes to do things. It can also get you into trouble when you're too trusting or naïve with other people's less than holy motives. My intuition has really served me well in these situations, when I've had to take a step back and assess if an opportunity is purposeful and meant for my highest good or if I'm just wishful thinking.

Balancing optimism and hope with your inner guru and guidance is the key to finding motivation, hope and happiness. It also keeps you from unnecessary risk. It's OK, and in fact empowering, to say NO and one of my favourite teachings from Gabrielle Bernstein is that 'No is a complete sentence.' You don't need to give an explanation if something feels wrong to you, just say no.

Optimism serves us well

It's good to expect good things and to view your world in a favourable way. Why not choose to feel good? We spend so much time torturing ourselves inside our minds that we waste precious time where we could be enjoying life instead. We are only here for a short time, so why not feel good and enjoy it!

All too often we spend time worrying about what may or may not be, and we waste our time and energy on projecting forwards in a negative way. Through optimism you can make your future projections more positive and use them as a motivator to keep you going, so you can feel more joy in your experience along the way. It's good to see good things and to expect good things to happen – through focusing your thoughts and intentions on these things, you're able to change the way you see life.

In black and white, you can choose to assume that bad things are going to happen, in which case it is likely more bad things will happen. Or, you can choose to assume that good things are going to happen and allow this to be the case. You can temper your expectation through coupling your optimism with the ability to let go of attachment to an outcome – and we'll be looking at how this can be helpful when manifesting visions tomorrow (see Day 19, page 139).

Be it until you see it, but also remember to keep it real and make sure you're supporting your optimism with positive steps in the right direction. It's good to be optimistic before you feel fully ready to embrace it, but it's even better to work on embodying the optimistic feeling, so that you do fully feel and believe it. This way, you can connect with your personal power within to really drive forwards with that positive knowing on the inside, which supports your optimistic thought.

#NOWISYOURCHANCE DAILY PRACTICE: THE BEST POSSIBLE SELF-POSITIVE PSYCHOLOGY INTERVENTION

Complete the Best Possible Self Positive Psychology Intervention by setting aside 15-20 minutes today to connect with how you and your life will look in the future, when everything has gone as well as it possibly could. This written exercise is also supported by a 'best possible self' guided meditation, which you can find at www.niycpidgeon.com/resources. Use the meditation as often as you need to over the coming weeks to support your shift into a more positive mindset.

###

— Day 19 —

DREAM BIG, DARLING

'Create a vision of who you want to be, and then live into that picture as if it were already true.'
ARNOLD SCHWARZENEGGER

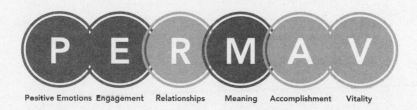

Positive Emotions Engagement Relationships Meaning Accomplishment Vitality

Our minds were born with wings to help us soar above reality and visualizing your future really can help to bring it into your reality. In fact many athletes, psychologists, big thinkers and entrepreneurs use visualization to help them connect with and create success.

In sport it's referred to as 'mental imagery', because getting clear on your goals and being able to build a picture of them in your mind's eye allows us to connect with them so much more powerfully. The act of moving into an altered brain state allows us to call up visual representations of our desires more easily. From this state we can embody the feelings of what it feels like to have achieved our goals, and then root this feeling and knowing deep into the subconscious, supported by positive beliefs.

Visualization: A life-changing tool

Visualization has proved to be a life-changing tool for me, but the first time I really became aware of its power was when I was standing in my living room in my apartment in Holland in November 2012, a few days before moving out and heading home to the UK. I was looking around me, when it suddenly dawned on me: this was the apartment that I'd been visualizing since I was a little girl. I remember saying to Mum and Dad, 'When I'm older I'm going to live in an apartment with a whole wall made out of glass,' and that's exactly what I realized I'd been living in for the past year. 'Wow,' I thought to myself, 'I manifested this.'

There had been no question that my desire wouldn't become my reality, but I didn't know how: I just set the intention, released it to the universe and continued on my path. As I got older I started to keep a list of my desires in the notes section of my phone, writing down everything that my heart desired, whether it was a feeling or an experience or something material.

Similarly with my vision board, I would take a few hours to find images and words that inspired me and connected me with the highest version of myself as I saw her in that moment. On my vision board went countries that I wanted to visit, pictures of magazines I wanted to write for, ideas for my TV shows and books, as well as my favourite cars, houses and watches. Recently, I realized I'd been writing in my mindset book every morning for the past nine months about my vision of waking up in my ideal Malibu home that overlooks the ocean and I woke up right there in that vision, which had again become real.

Learning to dream big

Given the above, I think it's pretty clear that I'm really huge on vision and I find it easy to dream big. But I also know what it can feel like to close your eyes and try to conjure up a vision for yourself, and be greeted by nothing but a blank canvas inside your mind. The following process is designed to help you get super clear on your vision and it's really super simple. Your vision is about feeling and meaning and connection, instead of wanting and grasping and desperation. You start by getting crystal clear on what it is you desire. If you don't know what you want and are working towards, then how on earth are you going to get there? The universe doesn't like mixed signals, so you had better make sure the message you're sending is clear.

#NOWISYOURCHANCE: CREATING YOUR VISION

There is a connection between mind and body, which means when we write we allow parts of our consciousness to flow that may not be as easy to tap into when you just sit and think. So to create your vision, use the following process:

1. SET YOUR INTENTION

It's important get clear on your vision, so start by writing down your answers to the following questions:

- When you think about your future, what do you see?

- What is your dream? Your goal? Your big vision?

Be bold here and set your sights higher than you ever have before.

Once you have written down your intention, make sure that it feels true for you, and that it resonates with your gut instinct and intuition. You might feel this connection in your heart space or in the solar plexus area, which is known as the second brain. It's important to attach feeling and meaning to this intention to give it extra power.

Now without judging your vision, write it down. Simply allow whatever is meant to come onto the page. Just let it flow out.

Once you have your vision down on paper, start to make it clearer. Hold the image of your vision in your mind's eye as you close your eyes and focus your attention upwards, and in between your eyes at the brow point (see Day 23, page 171). This is your third eye chakra, which allows you to connect with your vision, your higher consciousness and self. Make the details more detailed, and allow the image of your vision in your mind's eye to grow bigger, brighter, louder and more colourful.

It's also important that you set your intention. At this point, don't worry about how you're going to make your vision real. When you get caught up in the how, you can actually end up blocking your desires from manifesting. So many times I see people cancelling out their positive visions, by defeating themselves before they've started.

'I desire a home with a huge, brightly lit kitchen and five bedrooms, which is filled with laughter and people dropping by to socialize.' So far so good, right?

Then they ruin it by continuing, 'But I know that's way off in the future and I don't even know how that's going to be possible, because right Now I'm struggling to pay my rent on my three-bed place and I'm working so hard already.' Whoa! Stop!! Set the intention, put it out there and just like I did as a young girl, let it be.

2. ADD IN EMOTION

Next up is to attach emotion to your vision. Check in with yourself that this vision is truly what you desire. Engage all of your senses to experience your vision in real time. Feel the emotions that you'll feel in your vision, and feel connected with the inner strength, knowing and personal power that you are. Consider the emotions that you feel as yourself as your vision is manifest and understand that your vision isn't something that's to be achieved way off in front, it's actually happening right Now. I even like to imagine my vision as if it has already happened, in the past. This allows even more ease of connection with the emotions and helps you to believe you're there before you experience being there in the physical.

3. TAKE ACTION

Believe it or not, you do actually have to do some of the work in order to make your vision real. However, this step of the process is probably not what you might think. I'm not encouraging you to bust your ass, stress out or frantically try to get to where you want to go. I'm encouraging you to point yourself in the right direction, and keep your mindset positive and open, so that you're aware and able to notice opportunities and indicators that present themselves as steps in the right direction.

Remember that if you're on a downwards spiral you're not going to be looking up and noticing all that's good. The universe is conspiring for you; make sure that you're matching her with your behaviours, too. Think about who you need to be right Now in order to access that vision for yourself. Remember: the action you take in the Now is what allows your vision to become real.

4. ATTRACTION

In order to attract more of what you desire, you need to be thankful for all that you already are and have. It's easy to get anxious about not achieving your vision and to hate on life in the Now. The more you can resolve that conflict between feeling abundant and feeling in lack, the clearer your signal becomes. Find gratitude in the process and give thanks for your vision, as well as where you are right Now. The frequency of gratitude and joy allows your vision to manifest. (Feel free to go back to Day 1, see page 3, and check in with your gratitude practices if you need a reminder.)

5. EXPERIENCE

This is where you'll start to notice your vision manifesting into your reality. Keep your state positive and your awareness open, so that you notice the signs and signals. Practise getting clear on your vision and releasing your intentions to the universe – you might not get it quite right first time (just like me and my virtual palm trees), but as you practise you'll get better. Hold the vision and trust the process. Have a little faith in your vision. If you're emotionally connected and you're sure this vision is meaningful for you, trust that your vision will manifest. Ask that you receive the vision, or something better. When we speak this into our existence in this way, either our vision manifests or something better comes along that the universe has in store for us.

6. BRINGING YOUR VISION INTO REALITY

As you become more self-aware, and connect in with what you desire by attaching an image and emotion to your vision, know that the universe will rise up to support you. As you get clear and connected, you allow for the creation of more meaning and purpose in your life.

It's useful to stop and check in with where you're at, to reflect on what has gone well with your progress towards your goals and dreams, and how that made you feel. Also be transparent about what didn't go so well and how that made you feel, and what you might do differently next time to improve. This might involve taking out a notepad to explore your thoughts, or it might mean sitting quietly for a time just to think and allow the reflection to flow.

You might write out or meditate on a new vision for yourself, or simply notice where you have moved slightly off course and whether this feels right for you or not. Things might be going well – in which case it might be time to set some more, bigger, bolder goals to keep you motivated as you make progress. Or it might be time to reconnect back in with something that you're almost there with, but not quite experiencing in the way you desire to experience it just yet.

Whichever scenario you're experiencing, if you don't take time to connect, reflect, refine and realign, then you'll miss out on the opportunity to take action to correct your course, to find more that you love and desire, and to celebrate your happiness and successes when you realize you have them within you.

###

I found a 'best possible self' exercise that I'd completed years ago, when I began my career in positive psychology. It was so interesting to reflect on where I am at now, in relation to where I wanted to be at that time.

This is what it said:

> *Imagining myself as my best possible self, where things have gone as well as they possibly could, I am an international public speaker, a qualified positive psychologist and a chartered sport psychologist. I am happily married and I run my own business. I am surrounded by lots of family and friends, and I am a qualified pilot.*

So let's check these things out:

• International Public Speaker – Check!

• Qualified Positive Psychologist – Check!

• Chartered Sport Psychologist – No deal on this one. (Looking back, this was a goal set from ego, because I thought it would be a good title to have, meaning I wasn't connected to the goal.)

• Happily married – Not yet…

• Run my own business – Check!

• Surrounded by lots of family and friends – Check!

• Pilot – Not yet, but this is definitely still a goal of mine!

It was a real surprise to come across this exercise, and be able to notice how my goals and desires have evolved over time.

It was also interesting to see how I've achieved most of them, without even remembering that I'd specifically set them as goals! You might notice yourself do the same, where you come across a scrap of paper on which you had written down your goals and you now notice they've all been completed.

Nowadays I am much more mindful of my goals and my progress towards them. I like to set bold goals and then get creative with how to achieve them.

This process has worked powerfully for me, and has allowed me to grow and step into my own visions very quickly. Holding a long-term vision allows you to expand into that space. By ensuring non-attachment to the outcome, it means that you can benefit from the hope, optimism and happiness that's promoted through bringing your long-term vision into the now.

#NOWISYOURCHANCE DAILY PRACTICE: VISION MAPPER

Copy the following Vision Mapper into your journal to help you get clear on your desires and help them manifest into your reality. Then make sure you check in every day and make any note of any changes in how your vision is manifesting.

Intention	Get clear on your vision
Emotion	What three emotions can you connect in with?
Action	Who do you need to be?

Attraction	What can you be grateful for?
Experience	Where can you notice your vision is manifesting?

###

— *Day 20* —

GO TOWARDS YOUR JOY

'Find out where joy resides, and give it a voice far beyond singing. For to miss the joy is to miss all.'
ROBERT LOUIS STEVENSON

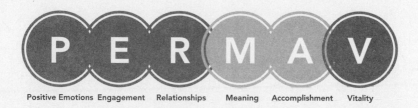

Positive Emotions Engagement   Relationships   Meaning Accomplishment Vitality

When we look up and around us, we begin to notice just how much we have to be in awe of – if we only take the time to look in the first place. In these tiny moments, we find joy. Nature provides an opportunity to take in the wonder of what's wonderful and good, through connecting to the subtleties and awesomeness of what is, without us forcing it to be so.

Simple activities such as getting outside for a walk, and setting the intention to switch on your awareness and notice all of the things that bring you joy along the way, can be a simple way to fill yourself up with moments of happiness. You're likely to know this to be true even if you don't know why, but studies have found that exercising can lead to benefits such as reduced stress, lower blood pressure and increased self-esteem,[1] as well as being effective at reducing anxiety.[2] It's thought that being in nature makes us happier because of our positive evolutionary reactions that connect us with Mother Earth and her capacity to support our survival, along with our ability to obtain electrons from the earth when walking barefoot to help us feel good. These moments can contribute to a broader sense of wellbeing and satisfaction. Choosing to do something that you love allows you to tap into that well of happiness every day. It's already there; you just have to wake up to it.

You might begin to notice and take in things that you hadn't seen before. Seeing a butterfly as it flies past you, noticing a leaf as it falls from a tree, taking in the blue skies above the clouds, or considering the enormity of our sun rising and providing us with light and heat are all moments that offer so much awe and joy. At the same time, they are moments that can be missed out on when we focus on the argument we just had, or the traffic, or how tired we are. Focus on what's good, choose to see through childlike eyes, and you'll experience the world and happiness in a whole new way.

#NOWISYOURCHANCE DAILY PRACTICE: DISCOVER MOMENTS OF JOY

Are you taking a moment to be in joy every day? To do those things that you love, or would love to do, if only you had the time, money, energy or any other excuse to be able to do them.

Choose to intentionally create a joyful experience today and leave your excuses behind.

###

Start before you're ready

To live your happiest life, sometimes you have to start before you're ready. Doing the things that you love – whether it's working out, writing or spending time with those you love – is so essential in designing a life that you love to live. Consider the things that you have been putting off that will really make a difference to your wellbeing right Now – are you harbouring a secret desire to read more, or to go to a new class, or paint, for example?

So why is it that these ideas so often fail to come to fruition? Why do we put our happiness out in front and tell ourselves that we are only allowed to experience it at a later date, but not Now? We create a gap between where we are now and where we want to be. This can only be closed by choosing to do the things that make you feel good Now, instead of grasping for things that you think will make you feel good in the future – and then feeling let down because you never do them.

What would life feel like if you chose to do something for you that allowed you to feel joy in the Now? You'd feel good, better, a moment of energy and connection to your higher self and how life can be, when you choose it. Finding happiness in the moment allows you to feel happier in general too. By savouring these tiny moments, you're able to realize that happiness is not about getting the best of everything, it's about making the best of everything you already have.

Connection to yourself, your environment and the things that bring you joy allows you to experience more joy as you move towards it. A life filled with joyful moments might not mean that everything goes well all of the time and, of course, that's impossible to create anyway. But when you know what allows you to tap into those joyful feelings, you know where you can go when you want to create more of them. So go towards your joy today.

I'm always sharing Happiness Hacks on social, which might include choosing to take the scenic route to work, even if it takes 10 minutes longer, or giving food, drinks or money to somebody in need. Little things that take little or no extra effort, but can create a powerful positive shift in the Now.

NIYC Notes

Playing I spy, for example, is a great way to increase your happy. Next time you have what I call 'grey time', where you would otherwise just be waiting or complaining about waiting (for example, when you're waiting in line or for appointment), say to yourself, 'I spy with my happy eye...' And look for all of the things around you in which you can find joy. You might become aware of the love between a mother and a child or notice someone holding a door open for another person. Seeing somebody else smile can help you to smile too, and by you making your grey time more playful, you get out of grump mode and enable yourself to stretch your enjoyment of an experience.

Reflecting on positive moments can also bring you more happiness – again by stretching your enjoyment! Recalling some of the hilarious experiences I've had with family and friends always puts me into a really good mood. For example, the time I heard a huge bang and a moan, and walked through to the kitchen to find my friend Natalie lying on the floor because she had slipped… on a cockroach! It so was hilarious that I can barely tell the story now without my stomach hurting from laughing! You know those moments that are so funny, but you really had to be there? Memories are amazing for allowing us to savour the moment – and we are always continually making more, too.

#NOWISYOURCHANCE: CREATE MORE JOY

Stretch your enjoyment of your joyful experiences by following the steps below:

Recall a time when you felt really happy and joyful. Write it down in your journal and then just close your eyes as you think about this time, calling up the positive emotions into the Now.

Think about a time coming up in your future when you anticipate feeling joy. Write it in the space below and then cast your mind forwards and feel in to that joyful experience, then bring the positive emotions in to the now.

Choose to savour something today. It might be finding awe in nature or it might be being extra present within a personal connection. Hold your joy in the Now and savour the depth of the emotion.

###

— Day 21 —

LET IT SHINE

*'I can do things you cannot, you
can do things I cannot; together
we can do great things.'*
MOTHER TERESA

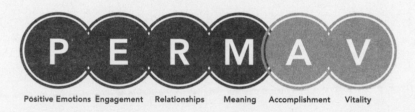

Positive Emotions Engagement   Relationships   Meaning   Accomplishment   Vitality

Conscious collaboration really floats my boat. I love to see how we can create when we join forces for a higher goal. Alone we have power, but together we are a force. Relationships, connection and community are all important in building a happy and thriving life, where they contribute to the experience of opportunities that enhance wellbeing, as well as fuelling thriving through buffering the negative effects of stress. Day 21 puts us smack bang in the middle of the PERMA criteria for flourishing is that 'R' for relationships, demanding our attention for their mindful nurturing.

They're not always easy, but relationships can be some of the most fulfilling elements of life, as well as our greatest teachers. At times we can feel alone, though we are never really alone, and we can find great comfort in connection. There are all sorts of relationships that make our world go round – from romantic partnerships, to colleagues, family and friends. Each has a different depth and dynamic that is magical in it's own special way.

In my own life I've very strong friendships built on understanding and trust, and I find it easy to stay open to new people and invest in the relationships I value. I don't believe in regret and I know that any relationship that has come to an end – romantic or otherwise – has served a purpose and is meant to be exactly as it is. You know by now that I'm a huge believer in intuition and when something doesn't feel right, it means it probably isn't, and that's when you need to stay true to yourself and the relationship with yourself.

 NIYC Notes

I've been in relationships where I've felt physically sick because I've felt unable to communicate what I feel. There have been times when I've got into a car with someone and felt my entire energy drain. More often though, I've had aches in my jaw and my stomach from laughing, and I've beamed with pride and cried in gratitude for the truly amazing humans in my life. Start to become aware of how your relationships make you feel. Start to notice what your intuition is telling you.

Where are you withholding?

Notice where you might not be giving your relationships the care and energy they deserve. Are you withholding love? Holding on to resentment? Not being present? What can you do more of? For romantic relationships, more attention, acceptance, allowing, appreciation and affection are needed to help boost and strengthen your relationship in a mindful way.

There is great joy in connection, and in feeling that spark of love and joy between you and another soul. Hugs are an easy way to get connected and a 20-second hug (with two arms instead of one as my mum keeps telling me!) releases the bonding neurotransmitter oxytocin, which helps to build trust and enhances the experience of positive emotions, too.

When I present on stage I ask my audiences to hug the person next to them and huge smiles break out around the room. When I ask them to hug that person again – this time for 20 seconds or longer – you can actually feel the energy of the room change and can sense the powerful connection in the air.

#NOWISYOURCHANCE: REACH OUT

Reach out to somebody you haven't spoken to recently and spend time reconnecting deeply with that person. This might mean making a phone call, suggesting a meetup, or FaceTiming from the other side of the world. Use this practice whenever you can make time for it.

###

Choose how you respond

A quick and easy way to invest in your relationships is by becoming more mindful of how you respond when someone shares good news. You can choose to offer an active, passive, constructive or destructive response. So imagine for a moment that your partner has just shared news about getting a promotion at work and then look at the table below to see how your response can affect your relationship. Focus on creating an active constructive response wherever possible.

Active constructive response	'That's great, you've earned it. I'm so proud of you,' followed by questions, which convey enthusiasm, support and interest.
Passive constructive response	'Great job, honey!' Then shift to the next topic. Like dinner.
Active destructive response	'Wow! Does this mean you'll be working later hours? Are they going to be paying you more? I can't believe they picked you out of all the candidates.' Just generally deflating.
Passive destructive response	Can take either of two forms: 'Wow! Wait until I tell you what happened to me today,' which is very self-focused, or 'What's for dinner?' and so ignoring the event altogether.

#NOWISYOURCHANCE DAILY PRACTICE:
UPGRADE YOUR RESPONSES

Hopefully, today's practice will become second nature to you, but to start with, become conscious of how you respond to others. Before answering, make sure you pause and really listen to the other person before answering with an active constructive response.

###

— *Day 22* —

CUT THE CHAOS

'It's all about finding the calm in the chaos.'
DONNA KARAN

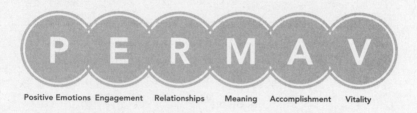

Positive Emotions Engagement   Relationships   Meaning   Accomplishment   Vitality

Multitasking is really just the art of being able to do lots of things, badly. Screaming to yourself that you can't find your keys in your handbag as you're running out of the door, late for an appointment, brushing your hair and talking on the phone at the same time, while also trying to forget that awful argument you had with your partner last night… Did you know that the brain can't cope with 10 things at once! Most of our brain function is happening in our subconscious, with the brain needing a lot of energy just to keep it going. That's why multitasking doesn't work – we simply don't have the capacity to give the energy to managing multiple things within our brains. As soon as you get out of busy, you'll find that you can get so much more done.

We often use being busy as an armour, a self-preservation mechanism, to block out the reality of needing to focus on what's real. If you're always busy doing something on the surface, then you don't need to pay attention to what's going on underneath and can become ineffective at getting the important things done. Now I'm all for taking action, but when you end up doing so much instead of being, you end up forcing the flow.

I used to notice myself saying, 'I'm so busy,' or 'I'm so stressed,' but what do those things even mean? Busy and stressed are labels that we give ourselves that consequently mean that we feel busier and more stressed – we take on what we decide we are. Living your happiest life is about being present to recognize that you're experiencing happiness along the way. You're not rushing through a few decades to arrive at happiness at the end – you're looking for the moments that you can experience right Now that allow you to connect with more joy and fulfilment and ease. Now Is Your Chance to be present. Now Is Your Chance to be in the flow. Life can be lived without it making you anxious and in fact, when you start to look after you more, your productivity increases and you get more done.

Even big business is waking up to the fact that to make your people and teams more effective, attention must be given to the person, as well as the process, with a very prominent piece of research showing the power of positive emotions for creating thriving teams.[1] Wellbeing in the workplace is not just a check box for corporate responsibility procedures, but a necessity when it comes to investing in people, and creating the biggest opportunity for personal and professional productivity, as well as profitability.

Choose how to respond

In my early 20s I would feel so frustrated when I couldn't find something, to the point that I would panic and cry. I didn't want to be late for work, but if I couldn't find my keys how could I get there?! Arghhh! I was living life in a stressed-out state that I was choosing! The situation would have been the reverse if I'd chosen to be calm and centred – and most likely I would have been able to locate my keys more quickly.

It's not the situation that affects you. It's the way you choose to respond to it. Every day you'll come across people, events or environments that have the potential to stress you out and your response determines what happens next. The person sat next to you in the office most likely isn't on the same journey of happiness and awareness as you, and nor do they need to be. As you focus on your own growth, happiness and calm, other people start to reap the positive effects, too.

One of my favourite observations is to notice how through one woman working on herself, and committing to her own happiness and personal growth, so many other people are positively influenced as a result. I would love to be able to quantify this ripple effect through some PosPsych research that could identify, for example, that if one woman invests in herself, and improves her happiness and wellbeing from a self-report score of 5/10 to 9/10, we see that the five people she spends the most time with also increase their self-report score, from a 4/10 to a 7/10.

I've seen this in action, where a client has empowered herself to work on herself in a personal mentoring programme with me for three months, much to her husband's disapproval. I've even had clients who have kept their coaching secret from their partners until they felt confident enough to share the positive results!

What emerges is that the newly empowered, vital and radiant woman is giving off such a positive new energy that the people around her, including the once-disapproving husband, are naturally shifted into feeling better and creating positive change, too. Stressed-out husbands become relaxed, happy and calm. Kids who are whining and moaning are enjoying more quality time and fun with their mum.

I want you to consider the potential of the impact of you doing this work for yourself, not just on yourself, but also on those around you who you have the opportunity to help, too. Letting go of the need to be stressed or choosing to take on life as a chore can help you to see life through new eyes and enjoy quality moments with those you love.

Want to live your happiest life? Let go of stress, make a plan and do the valuable things first.

#NOWISYOURCHANCE DAILY PRACTICE: CHECK IN WITH YOUR PRODUCTIVITY AND POSITIVITY

Go to www.niycpidgeon.com/resources and download the productivity and positivity planner shown below. Use it to highlight the items on your accomplishment list that are most important and most valuable for you to get done. Include on your planner:

- A list of your top three big goals and projects

- Your priorities

- Your mindset

- Your gratitude list

- Your learning

Check in with this document daily, and allow this tool to help you keep your eyes upwards to your vision and your feet firmly – and calmly – planted on the ground.

You'll feel happier, more organized, have greater clarity around your goals, a reminder of why you're working towards them and an increasing sense of accomplishment as you tick things off.

###

Summary: Daily Practices for Your Mind

Over the past 15 days you've been working with practices and interventions that promote positive thinking. Keep using the following daily practices to ensure you're on track:

- Express your truth

- Forgiveness affirmation

- Shift your mindset

- Creating a new reality

- Mantra of responsibility

- Supercharge your self-esteem

- Ask more questions

- Get mindful of your triggers

- Self-love mantra

- Support your goals

- The Best Possible Self-Positive Psychology Intervention

- Vision Mapper

- Discover moments of joy

- Upgrade your responses

- Check in with your productivity and positivity

Part III

YOUR SPIRIT

Spirituality is positively associated with wellbeing, and is defined as being made up of meaning and purpose, the will to live and faith in self, others and God. It's a universally recognized concept of a Divine force and something that's bigger than the self.

The body, mind and spirit are all interconnected, and taking care of all three elements is vitally important for our happiness. Having a spiritual practice such as meditation and considering yourself as 'spiritual' is linked with the experience of better relationships and social support, the ability to cope with stressful life events, and a greater use of other strengths and virtues such as kindness and forgiveness.[1] So Part III will be looking at ways to help you take care of your spirit and explore the more ethereal and transcendent areas of happiness, as well as positive psychology.

GO WITHIN,
SEE WHAT YOU FIND

*'You should sit in meditation for
20 minutes a day, unless you're too busy.
Then you should sit for an hour.'*
OLD ZEN ADAGE

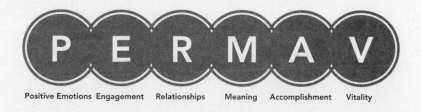

Positive Emotions   Engagement   Relationships   Meaning   Accomplishment   Vitality

M editation is the practice of calming and quieting the mind that creates a state of relaxation, and allows you to develop an intention for happiness or something else you desire. You might like to think of today's practice as creating your daily mental spring clean.

While meditation is still considered by many to be esoteric, the practice is actually grounded in vast amounts of science, both within and outside of positive psychology. Meditation is known to have many health benefits such as lowering stress, reducing blood pressure and the risk of cancers, and alleviating symptoms of depression and anxiety. It also has strong links with wellbeing, resilience and overall life satisfaction.[1]

Regular meditation practice can also help you to improve your focus, concentration and memory. It also supports happiness through the experience of these results, as well as by shifting your happiness set point. Sonja Ljubomirsky taught us through the development of the happiness pie chart that we all have a happiness set point.[2] A study found that after eight weeks of meditating once a day for an hour a day six days a week, participants reported that they felt happier. Follow-up tests found that participant's normal happiness set point had been raised. The practice of meditation in itself develops skills such as discipline and commitment, and might be associated with character strengths such as perseverance, kindness, spirituality and hope – it allows you to practise these strengths, as well as cultivate them.

But the real benefit of meditation is learning to pause in life and really be in the Now, as it can help you to gain greater awareness, more powerful perspectives, connect better with yourself, build better relationships and take a more proactive approach to life. Now Is Your Chance is a message to both take your opportunity to be in this moment, be fully immersed in it, find the glory and the joy in it, and to understand that Now really Is Your Chance, and you had better take action from this place and space, rather than put off your dreams for another day.

Illuminating the path

I opened my eyes after meditation one morning, and was surprised to see that the sun had risen and half of the class had left to go to work. I'd been chanting a mantra for 22 minutes and hadn't sensed a thing. You can be in such a meditative state that you're not aware of what's going on in this physical reality. Instead, you can be still in the quietness of yourself and the universe – a real gift to give to yourself.

Meditation has been key in illuminating my path, and amplifying both my happiness and my success. It has also allowed a sense of authentic power and presence to be built from within.

In our darkest moments, we can look to the light within to guide us. Though it's rarely this place that we choose to go. Instead we look outside, to see what quick fix we can find in our moment of desperation, wishing someone could take away the suffering we feel inside. If there were a single piece of advice I could give you when you're feeling fearful, anxious, worried or stressed out, then meditation would be it. You become more able to quiet the internal chatter of the monkey mind, and tune in to a sense of present calm, focus and allowing instead. This simple practice of training your mind and choosing a higher state of consciousness is available for everyone, costs nothing and affords you so much.

Mindful not mindless

The science of meditation and wellbeing within PosPsych supports the practice of mindfulness as a state of active and open attention in the present. Instead of being mind-less, you're mind-ful; aware and awakened to your experience in the Now, without judgement. As I described earlier, many studies into the benefits of meditation and mindfulness have shown that it can reduce worry, stress and emotional reactivity, and improve memory, focus and satisfaction within your relationships. So how does it work?

Meditation works by affecting the autonomic nervous system, which regulates organs and muscles, and controls functions such as breathing and your heart beating, and by altering brain waves from higher to lower frequency. This allows more time between thoughts, and greater awareness and intention around where you empower yourself to thrive. You move from a beta state into relaxation, and as your consciousness transitions to the meditative and visual mind, you come into a theta state.

There are five types of brain waves that help explain how meditation works:

- Gamma state (30–100Hz) – this is your peak positive state, where your mind is opened up ready for the intake and storing of information.

- Beta state (13–30Hz) – this is the state of the planning and thinking mind, and is where we spend most of our day.

- Alpha state (9–13Hz) – this more reflective state occurs during or after a relaxing activity, such as taking a walk in nature or practising yoga.

- Theta State (4–8hz) – in this state you transition from thinking to meditating and visualizing, and develop a deeper sense of awareness. You're more connected with your intuition and are able to tune out the noise, and tune in to what's important.

- Delta state (1–3Hz) – we reach this during deep sleep and Tibetan monks have been known to reach this state during deep meditation practice.

When you're in a meditative state, you're using alpha and theta brainwaves, which allows you to access the subconscious inner space, as well as remember your intuitions and insights that flow within your meditation.

Beginning a practice

Beginning a meditative practice is the quickest and most powerful way to drop the resistance surrounding you right Now – to let go of all that no longer serves you, allowing you to relax into yourself and who you truly are.

Your practice has so much power to save your life and help you to live your happiest life. With the wealth of scientific and experiential support, it's a mystery why so many are resistant to trying it. Through meditation we are always a student, even, and especially as, a teacher.

#NOWISYOURCHANCE DAILY PRACTICE: SIMPLE MEDITATION

If you're new to meditation you might like to start by adding just five minutes of practice a day.

1. Find a spot in your home or outside in nature where you won't be disturbed. Sit down, either on a chair or with your legs crossed, and your back up straight.

2. Bring your hands into your lap with your palms facing upwards in the receiving position.

3. Gently close your eyes and bring your attention to your breath.

4. Begin to breathe long and deep as you tune in to how your body feels right Now.

5. Continuing to breathe long and deep, with your eyes closed, turn your attention to your toes and feel how your toes feel right Now, with your feet resting on the floor. Notice any areas of contact or pressure and just observe, without judgement.

6. Move up to your ankles, your calves and your legs. Notice any stiffness, any pain, and how your legs feel.

7. Turn your attention to where your body connects with the chair or the floor and feel the weight of your body as it's supported. Feel how your fingers feel, and your hands, and your arms. How does your stomach feel, your chest, your shoulders and your neck?

8. As you check in with each area here, notice any areas of tension or tightness. As you continue to breathe deeply with long breaths, imagine breathing into any spaces and places of tension. As you breathe out, allow all of that tension to flow out with your breath.

9. Turn your attention to your mouth, relax your jaw and feel how your ears feel, your eyes, your nose, your forehead. Continue to breathe deeply here for a moment, fully conscious and present in how you feel.

10. When you're ready, open your eyes.

###

Creating mental stillness

Through good times and bad, meditation has been one of my go-to tools for not just surviving, but also truly thriving. I now meditate two or three times a day and teach meditation within my coaching programmes to help clients.

My first experience of meditation was as part of a project for my Masters degree, in which we were asked to choose five PosPsych interventions to test on ourselves and keep a self-report journal about our experiences. I remember feeling frustrated as I wrote up my assignment, deciding that meditation 'just wasn't for me'. I was busy in life as well as inside my mind, and sitting quietly trying to think about nothing just wasn't cutting it. What I didn't realize was that meditation was exactly what I needed; I was just going about it the wrong way. Instead of finding a meditation style that worked for me, I'd been sitting on the edge of my bed, trying to think about nothing. Hilarious.

Of course, when you try to think of nothing, every single thought in your mind seems to rush in. What worked for me was to practise meditation through guided YouTube meditations, meditation apps (I love Abraham-Hicks) and collective meditation in class.

I learned its true power one night when I was feeling so much pain, worry and confusion. After Googling my way through dozens of different websites, articles and videos, I was led to a meditation download that literally brought me to tears, as I felt a huge dark cloud leave above me.

Kundalini yoga

As well as simple meditation practice, I'd also like to encourage you to consider starting Kundalini yoga, as I've found this practice to be hugely powerful in providing me with the space for my love of meditation to grow.

Kundalini is an energy thought to be stored at the base of the spine. The practice of Kundalini yoga is to awaken the energy, and awaken your consciousness, develop your intuition and increase your experience of happiness. It's said that when you practice Kundalini yoga, you'll never be the same again.

> *The primary objective [of Kundalini] is to awaken the full potential of human awareness in each individual; that is, recognize our awareness, refine that awareness, and expand that awareness to our unlimited Self. Clear any inner duality, create the power to deeply listen, cultivate inner stillness, and prosper and deliver excellence in all that we do.*
>
> KUNDALINI RESEARCH INSTITUTE

Over the years, Kundalini yoga has helped me to release pain, trauma, hurt, anger and shame that I'd hidden inside of me for so long. Every class that I went to and every meditation helped to release my emotions, and has taught me that the more we let go, the more space we create to grow.

NIYC Notes

Each Kundalini class offers a different focus and a different pattern of exercises to work through, with one of the first principles of the practice being, 'happiness is your birth right'. No two teachers are the same and no two classes are the same. I am grateful to have been blessed to learn from some of the most amazing teachers on our planet. Having practised Kundalini with teachers in England, Spain, New Zealand, Australia, Bali (and also on my own in my bedroom), I am now a student in Los Angeles.

A typical 90-minute class starts with an introduction from the teacher, and spiritual insights or stories from the teachers' experience or from Yogi Bhajan, who brought the practice to the West in the 1960s. This is followed by a warm-up and the Kriya (a set of exercises that changes with each class). The class then moves on to a meditation, which includes chanting a mantra along with a hand mudra, and ends with a Savasana relaxation.

Through Kundalini yoga I've built the courage and inner strength to leave relationships that were no longer serving my highest good. I've found faith in myself, and in higher wisdom and guidance. I've also become more connected and confident on my path. I've had clearer thought processes, calmed worries and anxieties, and have even manifested tens of thousands of dollars through focused practice. I know that if I am feeling out of alignment, Kundalini will bring me back to me. It grounds me and reminds me not to believe my own bullshit, whether that be the ego story or the negative twists and turns that the psyche can so easily confuse us into.

Kundalini is not your run-of-the-mill type of yoga and meditation practice, and an open heart and mind is encouraged when you step through the door. Some of my most memorable moments include marching around the room shouting, staring into the eyes of a stranger while chanting, shaking and dancing wildly, having so much fun, with my arms involuntarily moving during a gong bath in exactly the same way as my friends did. I also remember our 4th July class being filled with almost 200 people committed to their own happiness and spiritual growth. Chanting sounds weird – and granted, it might not be for you – but I encourage you to try it today. Head off to YouTube to find one that fits or use the following Kundalini meditation practice:

#NOWISYOURCHANCE: KIRTAN KRIYA

The following meditation, courtesy of Wahe Kaur Khalsa of Golden Bridge, brings a total mental balance to the individual psyche and the electromagnetic projection of the aura. Through this constant practice, the mind awakens to the infinite capacity of the soul for sacrifice, service and creation.

1. Sit straight in Easy Pose (see illustration opposite).

2. Close your eyes and focus your attention to meditate at the Brow Point (in the middle of your forehead, also known as the third eye).

Sit in Easy Pose with your eyes closed

On Saa, touch the first
(Jupiter) finger

On Taa, touch the second
(Saturn) finger

On Naa, touch the
third (Sun) finger

On Maa, touch the fourth
(Mercury) finger

3. Speak the mantra 'Saa-Taa-Naa-Maa' out loud for five minutes, then in a whisper for five minutes and then silently in your mind for 10 minutes. Keep your elbows straight while chanting. The mudra changes as each fingertip touches in turn the tip of the thumb with firm pressure (see illustrations on previous page):

    ~ On Saa, touch the first (Jupiter) finger.

    ~ On Taa, touch the second (Saturn) finger.

    ~ On Naa, touch the third (Sun) finger.

    ~ On Maa, touch the fourth (Mercury) finger.

4. Each repetition of the mantra takes three to four seconds. The duration of the meditation may vary, as long as the proportion of loud, whisper, silent, whisper, loud is maintained.

5. Follow with one minute of stretching your arms over your head and spreading your fingers wide, shaking them out, circulating the energy, inhaling and exhaling three times.

6. Relax.

###

— Day 24 —
BE WITH YOUR INNER GURU

*'The intuitive mind is a sacred gift and
the rational mind is a faithful servant. We
have created a society that honors the
servant and has forgotten the gift.'*

ALBERT EINSTEIN

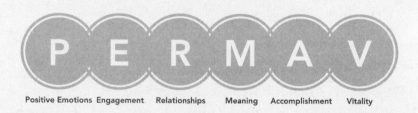

Positive Emotions Engagement. Relationships   Meaning   Accomplishment   VItality

I've spoken quite a lot about how my intuition has guided me
to create my life and you may have found yourself tuning in
to your intuition more easily as you've worked through the first
two sections. But today I'd like you to go deeper and start to
really tap into your inner knowing.

Your intuition is your ability to understand something without
logical reasoning and it's often described as 'gut instinct'.
Craving answers from someone else or wishing for somebody

else to tell you what to do is likely to lead to you feeling stuck or living a life you didn't choose. When we allow other people to make decisions for us, or get swayed by their opinion when it doesn't feel right, then we can wind up making decisions that aren't true to what we need. Inspired action to create a life you love is about learning to trust yourself and it's something that comes from deep within you – from your intuition and inner guidance, or your inner guru as I like to call her. In this chapter you'll learn how to tune in to her dulcet tones…

I feel my intuition as a wave of goosebumps all over my body, usually from the crown of my head and all down my arms, and I take it as a sign of spiritual confirmation that I'm on the right track. You might notice it as a feeling in your stomach or as a wise voice from deep within your heart. By this point in your journey, your self-awareness will have increased so much that you can really start to hear and feel what's true for you. You always have a choice in a moment and it's important to remember this when making decisions that feel right. Intuition can keep us safe and help us to move forwards on the path that's meant for our highest good.

Connect with your inner guru

To get connected with your own inner guru, first eliminate the noise and distractions that keep you occupied with thinking instead of feeling. Practically this might mean removing yourself from a situation and taking a walk or meditating (see Day 23, page 171), which will really help you tune in and hear what your intuition is guiding you towards. Be super honest with yourself about what you're feeling and don't worry about pleasing other people – you'll only come to regret it further down the line if you make choices that don't support you. Ask yourself how you'll feel a month or a year down the line and what your trajectory looks like based on the choices you make. Then journal your feelings and experiences, and notice what feels flowing and true. Writing can support you in connecting with your intuition and can allow your truth to come through.

When we learn to tune in to what we need and live more purposefully, we start to experience more enthusiasm for living. Interestingly, the word 'enthusiasm' comes from the Greek word 'entheos', meaning 'the God within'. The more we can tune in to enthusiasm and follow our joy, the more able we are to move forwards freely on our path, without weighty decisions on our shoulders that keep us stuck, and prevent us from living happily and with purpose. Within each of us lies the infinite potential to be, do, create and have all that we desire. But we need to learn to learn to trust ourselves and face down fear in order to create our path, instead of being pulled in a direction we don't want to be. You might think that not listening to your intuition one time will be OK, and won't really make a difference to your life and the way you feel. But, over time, you can find that you're not where you want to be, based on the choices you made or allowed other people to make for you. To create on the outside, we need to get on the frequency of gratitude and joy, and feel love and abundance on the inside first. This raises your vibration, and means you can connect with your intuition from an authentic and positive place, and listen to what your inner guru is telling you. Get mindful, get in the Now and you'll hear her.

You can distinguish your intuition from fear by noticing the thoughts and feelings you have when you're faced with making a decision. Fear will come up as a worried feeling and you might notice you play out 'worst-case' scenarios inside your mind, projecting forwards into the future about what might go wrong. Your intuition, on the other hand, will give you a sense of empowerment and knowing, and will have a more grounded energy to it. You'll feel less emotionally charged when you act from intuition and you'll be more focused on the present 'feeling' than 'thinking' forwards to the future with fear. Your future can actually be masked by fear, which is why it's important to be able to tell them apart. The more you practise tuning in to your intuition, the easier it will become to do so in the future, too.

Apple founder Steve Jobs famously said that 'intuition is a very powerful thing, more powerful than intellect', which is a comment that's also backed up by scientific studies. For example, in a study of car buyers, those who made quick, intuition-based decisions were satisfied with their purchases 60 per cent of the time. In contrast, the buyers who had weighed up all of the options methodically and made a decision out of rationality, were only happy with their purchases 25 per cent of the time.

When you learn to tune in to your inner guidance system, you'll find that what starts out as a whisper, turns into a roar and if it's ignored we end up in trouble. But when we listen to our inner guru whispers we hear what she is really saying and can follow her guidance onto our path for the highest good.

Tuning in

With practice and time, I've learned to listen to that whisper, even before it becomes a roar, and to take action based on trusting myself and what my inner guru is telling me – even if it means overcoming fear.

In particular, I remember the moment in November 2015 when I boarded a plane from Australia to head off on a 30-day around-the-world speaking and coaching tour. I'd always wanted to travel and do what I loved, speaking on stage, and hosting events and meetups with coaching clients. Because I'd powerfully held this vision, it was something that I intuitively knew I felt good about stepping into. I'd planned a trip that stretched from Australia to Los Angeles, Orlando, London, Newcastle, Dubai and Bali, but in the airport I felt scared, even though I knew it was the right thing to do. I knew that the trip would help me to expand, learn and grow, and that I could help so many people through my work. I was always going to make the trip – but it didn't stop me from feeling the fear and wondering what I was doing, travelling around the whole world on my own! The important thing was that I was able to see the difference between my fear and intuition. I understood that while my fear was saying no, my intuition was definitely telling me to go; though I did send my dad a message from the departure lounge saying that I was scared!

In contrast, when I've explored collaborations with partners for projects in business, and everything looks good in theory and on paper, I've still had a gut-wrenching feeling that something is wrong. I've honoured that feeling inside of me and you know what? Once you make the decision that it doesn't feel right, all of your energy will come back to replace the lethargy of having uncertainty and conflict hanging over you.

NIYC Notes

Of course, it can be good to ask for help and advice, too. I work with some of the best coaches and mentors in the world, and call upon my higher self, God, the universe, angels and spirit guides to guide me. What's different about acting with intuition is that you determine whether or not the advice feels true for you and then you can act on it. I have friends who are experienced in the business world and friends who are experienced at being awesome friends. Sometimes I even ask them for advice and then ignore it when it doesn't ring true or resonate with my soul.

Learning to trust your intuition

How many times have you heard yourself saying, 'I knew this was the wrong thing to do' or 'I had a feeling beforehand that it just wasn't right'? You hear it in business – the most successful leaders profess that they know to go with their gut instinct. We talk about 'women's intuition' and the knowing that something is feeling off or out of alignment. So why do we sometimes choose not to listen? Quite simply, we think that we know best. Our mind thinks, and our intuition senses and feels. What we think we know might not always be true, and we build up a way of thinking and feeling that's dependent on previous patterns and evaluations built up over time. We are not always objective and, of course, we can often be wrong.

However, the more we can start to listen in for that which is ringing true for us, the more we can allow ourselves to expand and be guided by a greater knowing and intuitive pull away from what's out of alignment, and towards more purposeful pursuits. Think of your intuition like a hobby that requires practice or a muscle that needs to be trained. We have a deep well of resources within us, just waiting to be unleashed, and it's important to allow the space for these to be tapped in to.

#NOWISYOURCHANCE:
LEARNING TO TUNE IN TO YOUR INTUITION

When you're crowded with other things and if you've ignored your intuition for some time, your ability to gauge what feels right or wrong might feel like it needs sharpening. Using this practice on a regular basis will help to strengthen your intuition and you'll begin to notice when things are not in alignment for your path or purpose:

1. Start by asking yourself questions and tuning in to the answers from within that you receive.

2. Ask a question that requires a yes or a no answer, and gauge how it feels to say yes and to say no.

3. Allow your inner guru to guide you towards the answer that's true for you.

As you practise this technique of asking questions, and listening and feeling into the answers that come from within you, the voice of your inner guru will get stronger as you allow her to be heard.

You might feel it in your heart or in your gut, and as you become more mindful of how that voice shows up for you, you can practise acting on your intuitive hunches, by making decisions that support the guidance you have received.

###

Personally, I know when a decision isn't right because I feel sick in the pit of my stomach, my heart feels like it's screaming at me, and I often feel tired and get a headache. All physical manifestations that mean my inner guru is saying no, instead of go! It's crucial that you also begin to separate a gut reaction from a fear response and learn to identify when your inner guru is guiding you towards or away from something, versus when you're being governed by fear.

Fear presents itself when you reach the edge of a comfort zone and you're challenged to venture into new territory. Your fear says no – but your inner guru might still be saying go. The subtle distinction may be characterized by your intuition providing a yes or a no response, where something feels right or feels wrong. Fear, on the other hand, is likely to show up as a feeling of not wanting to do something or of being scared to change something, and it's useful for you to check in with this. Notice where you have felt fearful of something and your inner guru has given you the courage to move on.

#NOWISYOURCHANCE DAILY PRACTICE:
INNER GUIDANCE

Each day spend five minutes noting down any guidance that you receive from your inner guru. Use this affirmation first to help you get present and tune in:

'I hear, accept and allow wisdom from my inner guru to come forth. I am grateful to be guided by my higher self.'

Then ask yourself:

- What decisions or choices can I notice right Now?

- What am I being guided towards?

- What is my inner guru guiding you to do?

###

Choosing to use your intuition more often will allow you to get more present and engaged with your life, and be more purposeful on your path. You'll feel more empowered, have a greater sense of calm and will be able to live your happiest life as a result.

— Day 25 —

EMBRACE YOUR PERSONAL POWER

'The empowered woman is powerful beyond measure and beautiful beyond description.'
STEVE MARABOLI

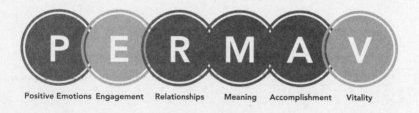

Positive Emotions Engagement   Relationships   Meaning   Accomplishment   Vitality

When a podcast host asked me, 'What's the best piece of advice you have ever been given?' I paused before answering, but not for long: 'To be myself and share my story.'

It might sound pretty basic, but when we try to find happiness through validation for doing things then we can only be applauded for so long. Sooner or later, hiding behind an exterior mask or story prevents our light from shining through.

Whether it's being a tomboy, hiding behind a theory or a set of beliefs, or being afraid to express your feelings, keeping up a facade of a persona is exhausting. We all create stories for ourselves to help us make sense and keep track of our life experiences. But our stories won't always facilitate living our happiest life and it can be easy to become stuck in a space – and stuck in a story – that doesn't serve us.

Self-awareness (again) is the key to observing your story and then choosing to break free from it. When we don't live authentically, we may end up not giving our best, because we are trying to be something or someone else. When you're yourself and lead from your heart – with passion, love and strength – you can be exceptional at all that you do, because you're being exceptional at being you.

Science of authenticity

The development of the theory of authenticity dates back to the 1960s with Maslow's 'hierarchy of needs', which presents the idea that we can improve our spiritual wellbeing once our basic needs of food, shelter, sleep and so on are satisfied. Being authentic is positively associated with higher self-esteem and greater satisfaction with life.[1] It also plays a positive role in leadership within organizations and businesses that are giving the nod to the value of openness as a powerful tool within the workplace.

In the millennial generation, we have seen an increase in the popularity and prevalence of realness, through mainstream media and magazines, reality television and, more recently, social media, candid video and live-stream stories, which offer the inside angle on people's lives. We are devouring content that shows the vulnerable side of celebrity and influence, where not everything has to be highly produced or polished and people are no longer afraid to speak their mind.

Authenticity researcher and author Brené Brown's TED Talk about the power of vulnerability has been watched 30 million times and I think that fact alone shows the relevance of this conversation in our present world.[2] Brené Brown states that:

> *Authenticity is a collection of choices that we have to make every day. It's about the choice to show up and be real. The choice to be honest. The choice to let our true selves be seen.*

Being honest about who we are can be challenging and bring us out of our comfort zone. However, honesty brings reward as we experience the sense of fulfilment and satisfaction that comes from practising being more authentic in every moment.

Authentic self-expression

Being able to express our wishes and desires allows us to feel and be heard, and to make purposeful choices along our path. But as someone who would only ever dress in black (think less Goth, more Jennifer Aniston), and in relationships would think something completely different to what I said, I know how it feels not to feel able to express yourself. I know through my healing work too, how it feels not to feel you have a voice and how it feels to have now finally found one – and an authentic one at that.

I used to become so frustrated when I wanted to say something and couldn't. It would feel painful inside of me, like something wanted to get out, and sometimes I would end up crying! We can create a fear around being ourselves and saying what we feel, through fear of upsetting others or making our situation less 'easy' to deal with. By wearing masks like this, we feel as though we can protect ourselves from judgement of our real selves, where people might find out we are not good enough or we are not who we portray ourselves to be – though in reality this only serves to keep us detached from experiencing true happiness and depth of connection. When you repress how you feel, it has an uncanny way of creeping back up on you at a later date, so why not practise new daily habits instead, where you can encourage yourself to speak your truth. Each time you'll notice you feel a little more empowered, and a little more relieved when you just get to be you, and don't have to keep up a charade or pretence.

Through healing myself and doing the deep spiritual work for myself, and deep emotional work with my counsellor – where I was forced to face up to who I was, my experiences and the way my life was looking at that time, as well as taking responsibility for changing it – I was able to build my strength moment by moment and day by day.

Each time I chose to include everyday habits such as meditation, journaling, giving myself space and time, and evenings off from my business to spend time alone to focus on how I was feeling, I knew I was taking a step towards being a stronger version of me who could use my struggle as growth. I was supporting myself in building a tougher mindset and connection with a vision of helping others. Because of this,

I've since been able to speak up, own my voice and embrace my personal power.

#NOWISYOURCHANCE:
EMBRACE YOUR PERSONAL POWER

I've often suggested through this book that happiness comes from self-awareness and this exercise allows you to practise this skill again. Through shining the light on where you feel empowered and disempowered, you'll be able to celebrate your small wins and successes (which can be so easily forgotten), and choose to make a change to support your happiness moving forwards.

Ask yourself the following questions, with the intention of being as mindful and honest as possible:

- Where can you remember feeling really accomplished at something?

- Where can you remember feeling really happy?

- Where can you remember feeling really confident?

- Where have you been really strong?

- Where have you been giving away your power recently?

- What would you love to feel able to say that you haven't yet felt able to say?

- What boundaries or personal commitments can you choose to make to yourself to claim your power back?

Write down your answers and observations, and send love and gratitude to yourself for being authentic and for all that you are. You can use your answers from these questions to help you see where you can further empower yourself within your life and relationships, and what positive feelings and emotions are available to you when you do so.

Make a commitment to take a small step that helps you to feel empowered today. This might mean practising saying something you desire to say, having a conversation you've been putting off for a while, celebrating a success that you've been too humble to share or committing to be more 'you' on your next Facebook Live video.

###

The world needs you

Believe it or not, the world doesn't need more clones or more sheep. The world needs you in all of your glory, and that means speaking your truth, standing in your power and claiming your worth.

Speaking about sharing how much I love waking up every day and just being myself in that podcast moved me to tears. As you embrace every part of you and really allow that to shine, you open up a space where joy can flow in. Where you're able to love the things you love, be the way you want to be, and know that even if you sit and do nothing at all, you're always more than enough.

Living your life authentically without limits means knowing that you're OK, able and giving the best of you. One step at a time, one person at a time, we are able to create a world that lives with joy and contentment, able to speak with truth, from the heart and without judgement.

Being more self-aware is not wizardry. It starts with you and is about setting a daily intention to take small actions that create the change. As that energy becomes more familiar, you'll discover that other people love you being yourself. They'll actually thank you for it! As humans we connect powerfully through story and vulnerability. We don't want to see someone pretending to have it all figured out! Nobody ever does! Through owning your stuff and opening up you become empowered – you can understand yourself more and allow others to understand them more, too. What's more, you may find a great peace of mind in being able to flop into bed at the end of your day and say, 'Yeah, I did my best today and I was myself all day long. I'm happy with that.'

You can find fulfilment in being yourself, acting with integrity and by letting go of the need to be something or someone else. No more worrying about something you said or didn't say! Embrace who you are. That in itself is empowering.

#NOWISYOURCHANCE DAILY PRACTICE: AUTHENTICALLY YOU

Who are you when you're your most authentic? Write down a list of all of the characteristics you notice about yourself when you're being your truest you. This might include things you do, the way you stand or sit or move, particular words you use, how you feel and also what you don't do. Then choose one element from this list to put into practice each day, so you can notice the progress you're making as your authentic self.

###

 NIYC Notes

If you have trouble speaking up for yourself, try starting conversations by saying, 'I've got something I need to say.' You may find it takes off the pressure of needing to blurt out the entire thing and means you have a way into the conversation.

As you become comfortable with speaking your truth, you'll feel yourself growing and feel a sense of accomplishment. You'll experience a sense of satisfaction, and increase your self-esteem, positive emotions and wellbeing. Because you're able to communicate more effectively, your relationship with yourself and others can be improved, too.

You're beautiful and amazing and fun and filled with light and love, and have so much to give for others, the world, and yourself. You can choose to be anyone in the world today. Choose to be authentically you.

— Day 26 —

WHAT'S LOVE GOT TO DO WITH IT? (EVERYTHING)

'Love is the absence of judgment.'
His Holiness the Dalai Lama

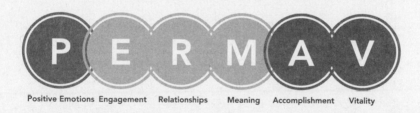

Positive Emotions Engagement Relationships Meaning Accomplishment Vitality

Most people say that you have two choices – to choose love or fear. I say we have one choice and that's love – fear is just an illusion sent to test us. If we allow the things that scare us to trip us up, then we will never make the progress that's possible for us when we choose to break through our limits.

Each time you make a choice, think about whether you're making the choice from love or from fear? Are you sending a signal that you're stepping up or shying away?

When we live in fear we live in the realm of low-level emotions and consciousness. When we live with the supreme emotion of love, we open ourselves up and each act of love allows us to embody happiness, to feel it grow within us, as we take a step further into living our happiest lives.

Now love isn't always the easiest place to lead from, and it takes a certain sense of awareness and level of consciousness to even become aware of when you might be acting or thinking from a place of fear.

Distinguishing between love and fear

Marianne Williamson said, 'Everything we do is either an act of love or a cry for help,' and offers us guidance on how we can begin to identify between the two. Leading with love and compassion for another and for yourself is not a sign of weakness. On the contrary, it's symbolic of your strength and commitment to do things a better way. Love is an amazing thing and it makes sense to want to experience more of it, where currently we are not getting enough.

When you love someone, what do you do? You express that love. You choose to make choices in each moment that favour love over fear. It's hard. But it doesn't have to be. Relationships and connection are what make the world go round, but it's often questionable if we are even connecting as deeply, authentically and consciously as we could. We limit ourselves because we are scared. I know that I've limited myself in this way in the past. I can see that there have been times and places where I've built walls around myself and cocooned my heart to prevent anyone getting in. Romantically, I've been called cold and too cool, and it's only through self-reflection that I've understood what's really been going on.

When we've been hurt, we don't want to be hurt again. But by avoiding pain or shame or rejection, we prevent ourselves from feeling the power of love. I know that many of my old behaviours were created from a place of fear and now I'm aware of that I can make more conscious choices moving forwards. There's so much that's possible. Feeling love with a complete stranger, when you share a smile or a gesture or a hug, is so wonderfully nurturing, allowing you both to fill up with that sparkle of happiness and energy. Supporting a friend, holding the space for someone to be heard, sharing a kiss or a touch and being honest when you know it's going to serve someone's growth – all acts of love. Acts of love in the moment, in the Now, where you can feel the reciprocated positive energy in your body and heart centre, through connection and knowing you care.

Self-love

But before we can truly love others, we need to understand how to love ourselves, and this is perhaps one of the biggest struggles that we face. Discovering self-love is a journey that's often first unearthed when we choose to acknowledge and awaken to the possibility that there is a better way to do things. If you're reading this book, you're already conscious of your potential to grow, and with that comes the potential to open up to both giving and receiving more love.

It's easy to mindlessly self-deprecate, self-sabotage or self-loathe, and much harder to consciously love, accept and honour all parts of us. We are wary of being considered big-headed or arrogant and often find it easier to brush off a compliment than to receive it graciously. To love yourself is not to be in ego or in fear. To love is to allow the true essence of you to shine through. You were made as love and all of the fear came later – through your environment, experience and unconscious choices. To receive love, you need to love yourself first.

#NOWISYOURCHANCE DAILY PRACTICE: CHOOSE LOVE OVER FEAR

So ask yourself: Where can you choose the most loving response today? How can you show your love for someone else today? How can you show some love for yourself today?

You might choose to remember that your workout or how you nourish your body are both acts of self-care. Or you might choose to do something special that nurtures your wellbeing, such as taking a long bubble bath or having a massage. However you choose to show yourself self-love, make this daily practice non-negotiable.

###

Healing through self-love

Through healing my past pain I was able to really see how little love I'd been showing myself. I'd been pushing my body, mind and spirit to the limit, engaging in self-destructive behaviours and relationships, and continually putting myself at risk. I'd been loving everybody else and trying to give to other people. I learned that to be able to shine brightly and help others, I need to fill myself up, and love and care for myself first. By taking some time for you and giving yourself the energy of love, you can be so much better than if you're depleted, self-loathing and afraid.

Loving yourself means showing up to do the work. It means investing in your personal, spiritual and physical growth. And it means committing to be the best version of you, no matter if the work feels tough – because you're worth it and the journey will be worth it. It might mean you have to do some soul-searching, to shine the light on what's been missing from you showing yourself that love. To accept yourself fully is to acknowledge that you deserve your own love.

 Commit to self-love

Through fierce commitment to self-love, my friend and client Ashley healed herself and transformed her life. Daily yoga and meditation, and deep journaling practices, as well as really listening to herself and her heart's desires, meant she swapped turmoil and chaos for a new life of connection. It took months of consistently showing up for herself, but through doing the work and loving herself first, she has been able to find her happy, build a new life she loves, start a family and make me super proud in the process.

#NOWISYOURCHANCE: AFFIRM SELF-LOVE

Today's self-care practice will help you to experience more joy and love, and allow you to develop a more nurturing relationship with yourself. You'll feel happier and more vital, and you'll even get a boost from the kind act of doing more for you.

List the things that you love about yourself – big or small, I want you to acknowledge them all. You might list qualities that you hold, such as being kind, funny or able to keep a secret, and include physical attributes – such as having soft hair, bright eyes or a strong body that can carry you through your day. By focusing on what you love *about* you, you affirm your love *for* you.

###

A friend of mine ran a pop-up restaurant and workshop in London. Scrawled on the blackboard wall on the way to the bathroom was the question: 'What's love got to do with it?' The answer? Everything! Love is the answer. Love is the key. Love is all there is. We get that Now! But what does it have to do with happiness?

The ability to give and receive love leads to feeling more satisfied in life – one of the key measures of wellbeing. Love is both a positive emotion and a character strength. We can think of love as being romantic, or caring, or connecting, and also transcending of these relational containers. Love can be felt in a million different ways and a happy life is one that's lived with more love. That much is clear. Let's live with more love – for others and ourselves.

— Day 27 —
BE IN SERVICE

*'Kindness is bigger than our
debates, philosophies and religions.
Kindness is universal.'*
DAVID R. HAMILTON PhD

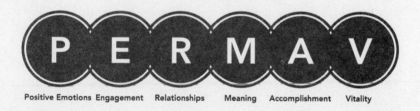

Positive Emotions Engagement   Relationships   Meaning   Accomplishment   Vitality

Yesterday we looked at love, and today we'll continue the
theme by looking at how we can get out of our heads and
into our hearts. Focusing on yourself makes it really easy to
get caught up in that negative self-talk loop that can bring you
crashing down like a ton of bricks in an instant. When we direct
our attention outwards and look at how we can help others,
our energy shifts into the positive and we open ourselves up
to a lot more happiness. Kindness is a positive psychology
principle, a spiritual teaching and a universal law.

Positive psychologist Sonja Lyubomirsky tested the effects of kindness in a six-week intervention, where students practised five acts of kindness – either spread across a week or condensed into a single day. Those who practised five acts of kindness within one day experienced a short-term increase in happiness, whereas the other students did not – showing that the timing of performing acts of kindness mattered.[1] In another study acts of kindness were assessed across a 10-week period and it was observed that doing kind things nine times each week versus three times had no additional positive impact on happiness. What did benefit happiness, however, was varying the type of kind act that was performed and these students showed an increase in happiness immediately after the intervention, as well as for up to a month afterwards.[2]

Kindness – a virtue and a strength

In PosPsych we look at kindness as a virtue and a character strength that everybody has within them, and can develop and experience additional positive effects from too. Since meeting Dr David Hamilton at one of our Hay House Christmas parties, I've been a huge fan. In his book *The Five Side Effects of Kindness*, he offers evidence for the positive side effects of kindness, which occur without you expecting them. The first of these five side effects is happiness, the other being the strengthening of relationships, slowing of the ageing process, dilating of arteries and benefitting your heart. It's also the best kind of contagious, too!

In religion, we notice kindness being passed down through the ages, where Jesus said to 'be kind to one another' and the Buddha encouraged us to, 'give, even if you only have a little'. The Dalai Lama helps us to understand the value of kindness as a core value, and as something that transcends and connects, instead of dividing, when he says, 'my religion is kindness'. When paired with the advent of positive psychology, and its ability to attribute a boost in wellbeing to the practice of kindness and provide a tangible practice to do so, we have been able to popularize and apply these age-old teachings to a greater extent.

Kindness is found through many universal laws too, as my friend and Doctor of Divinity, Erin Fall Haskell, teaches in her book *Awakening*. The universal law of harmony teaches that we are the cause and the effect of everything. When we act in a disharmonious way, those actions will flow out into the universe and ripple back to us until our harmony is restored. The universal law of grace teaches that when we give love and grace to others, we will receive the same in return. And we know from the law of attraction that, 'where your attention goes, your energy flows', so if you're kind to others you'll receive kindness in return.[1-2]

Doing the work on and for yourself isn't always easy. If you're working through something challenging, there will naturally be a few bad days thrown in along the way. Whether you're struggling to overcome trauma, working on your mindset or dealing with a relationship that's testing you, it doesn't have to mean you give up or abandon ship on your happiness. It just means you choose a different focus and pick up a different tool.

Let go of the need to receive

If you're struggling to feel happy, then doing a little something for someone else can really help. It doesn't even need to be a grand gesture or a gift. Simply asking, 'How can I help today?' can allow you to see the power in giving. I ask to be in service every single day and ask for guidance on how I can serve for the highest good of others. Living with this intention really allows you to open into a space where you see and feel abundance, and where you find deeper meaning in all that you do.

After deciding to work with a counsellor to help me process the experience of being raped, I spiralled into a hole of depression, worry and exhaustion, where I struggled to do normal tasks. I would wake up in the morning feeling like the smallest thing on my to-do list was a colossal challenge and I just didn't want to do it. It all felt too much to cope with. I decided to look at what was on the list that could really help someone else.

I'd been mentoring some start-up businesses at Newcastle University and had offered to help them with their business plan. I decided that instead of glancing over it and handing it back with a, 'It looks great,' I would dedicate an hour to really helping them as much as I could, working on my laptop from my bed. When I sent off the amended business plan with suggestions on how they could improve, I received a really lovely email in reply, to say the team were so grateful, and they had so much new motivation and inspiration to keep going. In that moment I could have rolled over and continued my pity party of how hard things were at that time, but by intentionally choosing to help someone right at the start of the day, I'd opened up my experience and shifted into a happy place.

Another time, when I was on a business retreat on Daydream, a tropical island off the coast of Australia, I made a point of collecting everybody's impact goals and missions. I totalled up the collective intention within the room and realized that in total, the intention was to help a minimum of 6,010,100 people and raise $1,103,100,000 for charity. Wow! When you focus on what you can create for others, you're able to create space for amazing things to be created and manifested. So much is possible when you build something bigger than yourself.

When you let go of the need to receive, and give from a place of love and creating value, you can see your reality transform in front of you. I used to panic about how many people I could get to sign up for my motivational speaking events. I would feel physically sick before I led a talk and would aggressively check my Instagram for likes after posting a photo or video. This all changed when I changed my mindset around giving. As soon as I focused on doing what I love, and how I can help people, my whole world changed and things began to flow. I began to create from the heart and with the intention of serving and lifting others. Now, before each coaching session or talk that I lead, I say a prayer to ask that the best possible service be delivered, for the highest mutual good. I learned to work from cause instead of for applause.

When I finally found United Nations Women after months of searching for a cause to support through my programmes and this book, and I learned more about the work they do through their campaigns to end violence to women, I actually cried with joy. I'd found a charity with which I felt such a deep alignment that I knew I would do everything in my power to help share the message and support their mission. Similarly, when I set up a volunteer park run in my home town, and stood in a field every Saturday morning for years to create a space for people to join together and experience thriving through movement and social connection, I knew it was a perfect fit and worth every freezing cold morning, because it created happiness in others and inside of me, too.

What can you choose to do today to make a positive difference for other people? How can you step up to make a positive change? When you're helpful, you're also more likely to be happy, as kindness is a powerful tool in not only helping others feel good, but in helping you to feel good, too. When you help others find their greatness, you shall find greatness, too.

#NOWISYOURCHANCE: CONNECTING WITH KINDNESS

Use this exercise to help you explore where you feel deeply aligned and called to practise a positive act related to kindness. This is often referred to in psychology as an altruistic behaviour, because it focuses on the welfare of others and might include pro-social behaviours such as volunteering, community service, helping others, comforting someone or intentionally sharing.

- What values do you hold as important?

- What experiences in your history stand out for you?

- What do you take a stand for or against?

- When you close you eyes and think about taking a stand for this message, how do you feel?

- What message are you prepared to stand beside even if it's unpopular to the masses?

- What cause or action might be a good fit based on your answers to these questions?

 NIYC Notes

People delete me from Facebook each time I post something that contains the word 'rape' and I would continually be asked why I was leading a park run without being paid or charging a fee. Even when your stance is unpopular with some people, when you're so aligned with the good you're here to create in this world, the haters really don't matter.

I invite you to let go of being focused on an outcome and instead focus on what you can give from the heart in each moment. When I meet someone new, I always ask, 'How can I help you? What do you need?' Quite often, people are surprised that I'm asking what can I give, instead of what can I get. Service and joy can be used as guidance to help you release blocks, find meaning and create value.

#NOWISYOURCHANCE DAILY PRACTICE: CHOOSING TO HELP OTHERS

Do something for somebody else today and expect nothing in return. This random act of kindness has the power to create a ripple effect of joy around the world.

Your random act of kindness might mean buying a coffee and paying it forwards by buying one for someone else, too. It might be helping someone to carry their shopping, leaving a note for a stranger to wish them a good day or taking care of the chores for a friend so they can put their feet up when they get home from work. I heard a story recently of a lady who owns a flower shop who makes up a bunch of flowers each week and leaves them in a different place for someone to find!

###

Who will you give a random act of kindness to today, and what will you choose to do? Kindness helps you to feel happier, more present and engaged, and to experience positive relationships. It also allows you a sense of meaning and purpose in your life. It gives you a hit of feeling accomplished, and helps your heart, your health and your longevity. From the universe, to religion, to the new science of happiness, kindness is a huge yes for you when looking to lead your happiest life.

Who can you ask, 'What can I help with?' Most people won't ask for help when they need it. By starting the conversation, you can be there and show you care.

— Day 28 —

ALL THINGS ARE POSSIBLE WITH PERSPECTIVE

*'Yesterday I was clever, so I wanted
to change the world. Today I am
wise, so I am changing myself.'*
RUMI

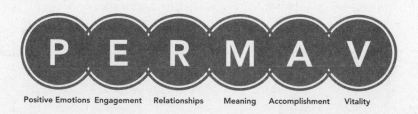

Positive Emotions Engagement   Relationships   Meaning Accomplishment   Vitality

When you take a moment to look, what do you see? Ask two people to recount their memory of the same experience and it's likely that each of them will relay a slightly different, or perhaps even contrary, version of events, as their perspective influences their report.

Think about it for a moment... How do you interpret and remember things? Is what you think happened, really what

215

happened? Will we ever know? Each and every one of us has a unique map of the world, and we are able to interpret and respond to new experiences based on what we think we already know. We form an opinion based on a prior experience and often it becomes just another layer of our story.

I was lucky enough to be in the presence of Dr Wayne Dyer at one of his last speaking engagements, just a few days before he passed. A favourite message he shares is: 'When you change the way you look at things, the things you look at change.'

Removing the filters (the illusion)

Just like a social media filter, we are constantly filtering and processing what we see and experience, building our own interpretation of what is. Imagine adding your new experience and perception on top of years of patterns and learned behaviours. It becomes easy to skew your judgement based on your non-objective view. Your interpretations and responses of an event may be too extreme or affected by other things that you have previously experienced. It takes for you to choose a level of consciousness that allows you to see clearly the opportunity within a situation and open yourself up to accepting the gift of growth.

Check back in with your growth mindset here and your ability to shift from taking a fixed mindset approach into a growth approach in any moment (see page 75). Your growth mindset can be used as a bridge to help you gain perspective. You can use it as a broad overarching life principle to help you raise your consciousness and awareness, and you can choose to use it in the Now, too. By taking a step back and widening the lens, you can choose to see things in a light that illuminates what you need to learn and it gives you power to grow.

Choosing how to respond

Living between two mini mansions in West Hollywood with other entrepreneurs working on awesome (and very different) creative projects, it was interesting to notice the impact of perspective on both behaviour and also upon the outcome of a situation. Human behaviour is fascinating and putting 14 entrepreneurs into a living space like this is bound to provide great material for a social experiment! On reflection I wish I'd installed cameras to capture things, *Big Brother* style! I'd been chatting in passing with one of the girls and she apologized for her tendency to fly off the handle when reacting to a situation. She had noticed that she had an extreme response and felt she needed to apologize for that. But why apologize for a particular behaviour, when you can do something to prevent it in the first place? Her reaction was disturbing to her, leading her to feel guilty and affecting others, too.

I spoke with her about our ability to choose how we want to respond to a situation and that it's not the situation that causes our reaction, but rather our choice to have that reaction. When we have the awareness that it's possible to choose to see things a different way, we are able to adapt our response, as well. Imagine life is like water, with a constant flow of experiences, and other people's actions, comments and ideas. Imagine them all flowing over you and around you, and not affecting you. When you imagine life like water, you're able to take a more neutral perspective that allows you more objectivity, less extreme reactions, and the opportunity to operate from a centred and grounded place.

Now when something 'bad' happens, I look at what the bigger picture view might be. I know that the universe is always conspiring for us and our growth. A curve ball is sent to try us, not break us, so that we can find a better way through. Looking back on my experiences to this point, much of the power in what I've learned has arisen through working through hard times. Each friend who passed away left a teaching behind which helped me grow, each relationship and break-up has led to more self-mastery and insight into what might be done better next time, and being raped has allowed me to find a greater strength in myself to see what's possible when we show up for ourselves and do the work.

We all have a story. We all create our story, in fact. Indeed, this is the story I've created for myself, joining the dots backwards, to build a book to share with and serve you. With each story we create for ourselves we have the opportunity to make it all about us and stay stuck in that story, or to make the choice to see our story with a perspective that allows our experience to be recognized as having wider value to help both ourselves and others grow. I always wanted to write a book; though it wasn't until I found the powerful purpose and message that can help so many people that I began to bring the idea into reality.

Time gives us perspective, but gaining perspective doesn't necessarily require time. When you commit to finding perspective in the Now, you're able to shift quickly into a growth mindset and choose to interpret things in a supportive, self-loving way. You can do it in an instant. Consider what's the most loving response you could choose. Notice your ability to mould your own interpretation of things, to understand your past, as well as write your future from the Now.

#NOWISYOURCHANCE DAILY PRACTICE: REFLECTION

Use this simple tool for reflection today and choose an experience that you're committed to finding a different perspective for.

For example, if your partner came home from work and he was in a bad mood, and you took it to heart that he didn't notice that you had cleaned the kitchen and styled your hair, and therefore snapped and sulked, how could you choose to view that differently and attach a different meaning?

Ask yourself the following questions:

- Which experience would I like to find a different perspective for?

- What was good about this experience?

- What wasn't so good about this experience?

- What learning can I take?

- What is the new perspective that I choose?

1. Choose to shoot yourself up in the sky and look down on yourself from above:

    ~   Ask yourself how impactful your current situation is on the bigger picture.

~ Ask yourself if it really matters either way at all.

~ Does the thing you're worrying about have a big influence on the world or on your life in 20 years' time?

~ The answer will usually be no.

2. Choose to take yourself out of the situation and look through somebody else's eyes.

~ Gain perspective through another set of values, another take on the world, another stance on the situation.

~ We realize that it's not as big or as scary or as stressful as it had first seemed.

3. Choose to ask yourself what your role model would do in this situation – what piece of advice this person might give.

~ How would Mahatma Gandhi act in this situation?

~ What would Richard Branson do?

~ Take strength from somebody else's wisdom and knowing that the next step is available to you.

~ A moment to allow for perspective is all that it takes to release worry and stress, and give yourself space and knowing of your next best step.

Use what you have learned in this exercise to help you find a new perspective anytime you feel challenged in daily life. The more accustomed you become to shifting your perception into neutral, the easier you'll find it to create new meaning.

###

GET SOME GRIT

*'I am not what happened to me –
I am what I choose to become.'*
CARL JUNG

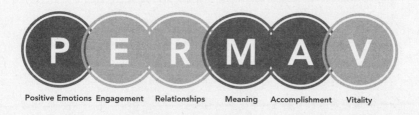

Positive Emotions Engagement Relationships Meaning Accomplishment Vitality

Remembering that all things are possible with perspective can highlight your ability to not just manage an adversity, but also bounce back from it and be even better as a result. The PosPsych concept of resilience is one that brings the journey of this book full circle. We started looking at how gratitude and the importance of creating a positive mindset is so important to our happiness, and can now add an extra layer to the importance of doing that.

Resilience is the ability to adapt to life when conditions are adverse. You either stand strong, waiver and bounce back, or grow as a result. We all demonstrate resilience at some time or other, whether it's the result of heartbreak, bullying, trauma, serious illness or struggling with health. It's not something that's extraordinary; although we do all have differing levels and coping mechanisms, which are strengthened when we feel fearful, distressed, confused or uncomfortable.

How resilience boosts happiness

Resilience is so important in helping us to thrive and live our happiest lives, because it's natural that life is going to throw us some curve balls along the way. Being resilient helps us to weather the storm. While it doesn't seem like the most exciting and energizing, it's so important to help ground you and keep you going. It actually draws upon many of the concepts we've already discussed in this book, such as having a growth mindset, staying hopeful and optimistic, and generating more positive emotions to help you build your psychological resources. You can develop resilience by choosing to take actions that support a solution and forwards motion, while maintaining a positive perception of yourself, and your ability to cope with stress and adversity, too.

Positive emotions will help you to regulate your emotions more easily and to find the positive meaning in what might otherwise be viewed as a negative situation or experience. Positive coping, positive affect and positive thinking are all elements associated with promoting resilience.[1] More resilience means less stress, a greater sense of self-confidence, improved relationships and the ability to maintain a positive view of the future. To gain more resilience what you need to do is focus on what you can do to work towards it – and let go of the things that you're not able to control.

In two studies carried out on daily stressors and emotions, participants were asked to complete a diary that tracked scores on the resilience scale with daily stressful events and the corresponding experience of positive emotions. The first study was carried out with a normal population of participants and the second with recently bereaved widows. Both studies found that the experience of more positive emotions was associated with a smaller reaction to, and a quicker recovery from, stressful events.[2]

Becoming more resilient

When I was staying in the UK with my mum during a week-long trip to present and speak at a few events, my schedule was so filled and I was so tired that it just didn't seem possible to get everything done. I was complaining and sneaking in minutes at a time to lie down and close my eyes. We ended up laughing so hard about how ridiculous it was that I had so much to do that we had tears in our eyes! 'You're a bloody whirlwind, Nicola,' she said.

When we laughed about my schedule and about how much I had to do, in those tiny moments of shifting focus and perspective, we were able to let the stress and tension go. As a result, we were able to carry on with renewed energy to keep things moving.

Resilience is such a big part of living your happiest life. Research supports the idea that life satisfaction comes from the building of psychological resources, the experience of more positive emotions, and the ability to dust yourself off and try again.[3] To become more resilient, choose to consciously take care of your wellbeing, commit to your growth mindset and remember that all things are possible with perspective. Being able to laugh in a stressful situation immediately diffuses the negativity and bringing in those broadening positive emotions can allow you to find a solution more quickly.

#NOWISYOURCHANCE DAILY PRACTICE: MENTAL TOOLKIT

Take a look through the list below and tick each activity you would like to be able to do more of in your life:

- Spending quality time with your partner

- Speaking to or doing something with your family

- Speaking to or doing something with good friends

- Meeting with others who share something in common (e.g. interest groups, support groups, faith-related groups)

- Spending time helping others (e.g. providing expertise, money, time, effort)

- Spending time on hobbies or interests (e.g. gardening, reading, following sports)

- Exercising or doing some other form of physical activity (e.g. walking, cycling)

- Spending time with a pet animal/animals

- Going on outings (e.g. going out for a meal or function, time out in nature)

- Going on trips (e.g. visiting family or friends, day trips, holidays)

- Spending quality time alone doing your own thing (e.g. relaxing, watching something, treating yourself)

- Doing something you find amusing (e.g. winding someone up, watching a comedy)

- Spiritual activities (e.g. praying, meditating, worshipping)

- Counting your blessings

- Framing things in a more positive light

- Working on something you get a sense of achievement from

- Doing something you find mentally challenging

- Devoting time to an important personal goal (e.g. a relationship, health, a holiday)

- Working towards achieving a property goal (e.g. grounds, new house, vehicle)

- Devoting effort to a work goal (e.g. cutting back workload, reaching a target)

- Working in a role that you enjoy (either paid or unpaid)

- Doing something that uses your particular strengths and skills

All the above activities are known to increase your levels of happiness. As you experience more positive emotions, you broaden and build your mental toolkit, meaning you're able to become more resilient as a result.

Remember: as you consciously choose to do more of the things you love, you experience the double benefit of boosting your joy, as well as being better equipped to navigate challenges.[4]

###

Going beyond trauma

Researchers Richard Tedeschi and Lawrence Calhoun at the University of North Carolina into posttraumatic growth (PTG) in 1995 showed how it's possible to rise to higher levels of psychological functioning after experiencing trauma. Where resilience sees us return to a baseline point, posttraumatic growth sees us go beyond our previous level so we can experience positive psychological change as a result of the struggle with adversity and the human propensity for growth. Posttraumatic growth is observed across progressive stages, beginning with intrusive thoughts about the trauma and progressing to self-analysis, finding meaning, and being able to accept the changed map of the world.[5]

PTG is noticed across a range of traumas, such as military combat, surviving cancer and sexual assault.[6] Kate Hefferon, my supervisor for my master's, has done some amazing research into the area of PTG. A qualitative study she carried out looked at breast cancer survivors and suggested that participation in physical activity can support the experience of growth post trauma.[7] It's thought that this effect might be more strongly associated with traumas related to the body, a theory that was further researched in 2015, with a study that looks at trauma associated with bodily injury and the unique elements to growth that occur as a result.[8]

My personal experience backs up the theory and I've found that surviving being raped has made me happier than ever. It has allowed me such depth of experience and healing that I now operate from a stronger and more optimistic place. I know I'm not alone in this, as it's suggested that 40–70 per cent of trauma survivors experience growth as a result of it. Posttraumatic growth is characterized by a stronger and more authentic sense of self, improved relationships, increased sense of purpose, changed priorities and enhanced spiritual beliefs.

 NIYC Notes

We can observe examples of posttraumatic growth all around us within popular media. For example, Oprah Winfrey was famously abused as a child, Kris Carr overcame cancer and went on to thrive, and Charlize Theron watched her mother kill her father and channelled the energy to fuel her success. Consider who you might look to as a role model to help you see the power and possibility for PTG. Even in the darkness, you can still find your light.

I don't want to suggest that trauma is a good thing, nor at all necessary when looking to live your happiest life. Rather I mention it to demonstrate that it's entirely possible – and probable, in fact – that you can live your happiest life despite it and even as a result of it.

#NOWISYOURCHANCE:
FINDING HAPPINESS WITHIN TRAUMA

Use this exercise to look for the learning within trauma, to reflect on experiences that have challenged you in the past and to observe where you might have grown as a result.

Where have you been able to make your struggle your strength? Consider at least one experience that has felt painful at the time, that you can now see helped you in learning something and growing. For example, it might be a relationship that you let go of, which you now realise has helped you to gain an awareness of what's important to you within a partnership. Or it might be an injury or serious illness you overcame. Or perhaps weathering the storm of a rocky patch in business that allows you huge strength in making decisions in the future.

Ask yourself the following questions to explore the silver linings in the clouds:

- Which experience did I struggle with at the time?

- What did I learn from this experience?

- How did I grow?

Important note: this exercise is not a replacement for professional therapy, so always see a trained professional if you need help working through trauma.

###

Positive emotions facilitate building resilience, so you have an extra reason to decide to live your happiest life. This work doesn't just make you feel better, but it also helps deepen your understanding of the tough times. The experience of trauma can lead to growth through the finding of meaning within and after the traumatic experience, and associating it with a new lease of life. You're capable of amazing things.

GET IN A PEAK STATE AND RADIATE!

'It's what you do daily that matters the most.'
JIM ROHN

Positive Emotions Engagement Relationships Meaning Accomplishment Vitality

How you start your day has huge bearing on how you feel and how you can allow the rest of your day to flow – or not flow as the case may be. The minutes that you invest in the morning can give you hours back in energy, clarity and focus later in the day. I'm not asking you to spend hours with yourself – I get that you're busy, right?! What I'm asking you for is 20 minutes every day to commit to living your happiest life. You can do that, right! Whether it means getting up 20 minutes earlier, going to bed 20 minutes later or streamlining your current morning routine to do less of what's not serving you and more of what absolutely will, I encourage you to get 100 per cent committed to today's practice.

Your morning mindset ritual is your time to be and feel the way you've always wanted to feel, and the power of this ritual is threefold:

1. It helps you to get really present and grounded, meaning that you think more clearly, and feel calmer and happier for the rest of your day.

2. You can manifest your desires more powerfully and reach your goals more quickly by connecting with how you want to feel and choosing to feel that right Now.

3. You operate from a peak performing state for the rest of your day with that extra sparkle and personal power.

The power of a morning ritual

The reason I recommend that you create a ritual in the morning is because that's when our willpower tends to be strongest. But it's even more important to commit to your ritual as a non-negotiable part of your life – just like brushing your teeth (but so much more fun). Think of it as your opportunity to show your day what you're made of and if #NowIsYourChance needed a place to be practised, well darling, this is it.

The most successful people are the ones who build successful daily habits. And the happiest people? You got it – they build daily habits that fuel their happiness, too. These few things will make the biggest difference in your day, in the way you show up for yourself and your life, and your energy, productivity, happiness and personal power.

There are seven steps to the ritual I am going to share with you, and each step has an importance and purpose of its own. Your ritual will take you just 20 minutes, and I simply ask that you give it your full heart and intention so that you can truly shine.

Step #1 – Gratitude (60 seconds)

Begin with a grateful thought and start your day in the best possible way. By being in gratitude before opening your eyes or being fully awake, you set the intention for wellbeing and good things to flow in.

I start my day by thinking to myself, 'Thank you, thank you, thank you, thank you for this day. I am grateful in every possible way.' And then I continue with a gratitude rampage inside my mind, where I allow myself to be in gratitude for all that I am and have. This usually starts by being grateful for my giant comfy bed, and always ends with an internal smile and the knowledge that I've started my day on the right foot – and I haven't even opened my eyes yet!

Step #2 – Meditation (5 minutes)

You already know the why behind meditation, and Now Is Your Chance to put the intention into action and make meditation part of your daily routine. I always suggest starting small, so for your morning ritual I recommend just five minutes of meditation, using a guided YouTube meditation or listening to a piece of music that really allows you to turn your focus inwards. I love listening to Gurunam Singh, *Grace of God*, during my morning ritual. But whatever you choose to listen to, starting the day from a meditative space really allows you to create a sense of presence and personal power that sets the tone for the rest of the day.

Step #3 – Vision (3 minutes)

Connect with your vision daily (see Day 19, page 139). This is going to help you keep your big picture perspective in your mind and out in front, so that you know what you're moving towards. When you think of your vision each day I want you to make it clearer and clearer as you allow your future to become brighter and more detailed. Imagine how you'll feel as you visualize your best possible self, living your happiest life. Feel the emotions that you'll feel – I suggest you choose three and really focus on pulling up those positive emotions in the Now. You create through feeling rather than thinking, so the more emotion and connection you can create and attach to your vision, the more quickly and powerfully you're able to manifest it.

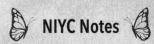

🦋 NIYC Notes 🦋

Check out my 'Best Possible Self Meditation' at www.niycpidgeon.com/resources and use this every day within the vision section of your morning mindset ritual.

Step #4 – Dance (3 minutes)

This is your opportunity to LET GO! Dancing used to be something that I felt sooo uncomfortable doing and Now I do it multiple times a day! Choose a song that you really love to boogie to and play it loud! Allow yourself to move, and feel the freedom that comes with owning your dance party and fully expressing yourself. If anybody saw me in the mornings they would think I needed to go to the loony bin, but I love this part of my day so much that nobody is going to take it away. Dance for one song and really go all out. Your dance party is your opportunity to express yourself and build your confidence in being you. The more crazy you can go at home in your kitchen, the more you'll notice your confidence in being yourself will grow in other situations, too.

Step #5 – Affirmations (2 minutes)

Select or create an affirmation that's meaningful for you. I choose my affirmations based on what I am working on at the time. I have some affirmations that I stick with for months and others that I might pick up for just one day. I like to create my own affirmations using inspired thought and if there is something that I am struggling with, or a persistent niggling thought that I wish to let go of, I will create something positive to replace it. In this part of your morning mindset ritual, choose an affirmation that feels true for you and one that you feel has the power to create a shift from where you are right Now. Write down this affirmation three times while really connecting with and feeling its meaning:

I love and accept myself first.

I give myself permission to be happy.

I choose to live with meaning.

I allow abundance to flow.

I am grateful for miracles.

I am committed to being my best.

Step #6 – Movement (3 minutes)

Get moving in your morning mindset ritual and shift that stagnant energy around your body. Find a song that really gets you energized and makes you feel that fire inside. Moving your body is one of the keys to being a thriving and optimally functioning human, so it's imperative that you make movement an integral part of your day.

In my morning ritual I move through sets of squats, press-ups, sit-ups and star jumps for the length of a song. I might also do a workout later, but I still always make sure I move my body as part of my morning mindset ritual. Sometimes I extend this part of my ritual to include a 20-minute Qigong session, or go for a run or to a spin class. For you, you might choose some yoga, or stretching – whatever feels true for you.

Step #7 – Nourish

Celebrate the completion of your morning mindset ritual by nourishing your body. I like to drink my green juice, and enjoy a healthy breakfast or protein shake. Eating breakfast rounds off your morning ritual, and makes sure that your mindset and body are both primed for your happiest and most flowing successful day!

This version of your morning ritual will take you no more than 20 minutes; though you might choose to extend it if you wish. I'll often extend my meditation and movement sections to support my mindset even more. The more present and connected you can be within your morning ritual, the greater your sense of self-control, and the more energy and productivity you'll experience throughout your day. Happy and successful people have the same 24 hours in their day – the difference is that they choose to spend their time differently and they invest in themselves at the start of their day. Be one of these people today.

#NOWISYOURCHANCE DAILY PRACTICE: MORNING RITUAL

Build your own seven-step morning mindset ritual using the table below... and then give it a go! I promise you'll be addicted:

Gratitude	What gratitude prayer will you use to begin your day? If you're not sure where to start, try, 'Thank you, thank you, thank you, thank you for this day. I am grateful in every possible way.'
Meditation	Which meditation recording or song will you choose?
Vision	Which song allows you to project powerfully into your chosen reality?

Dance Party	Which song do you LOVE to dance to?
Affirmations	Which mantras are important and powerful for you? You might choose to use the affirmations you created on Day 11 (see page 81) or something like this, 'Every day in every way, I am growing stronger, happier and more abundant.'
Movement	Which song will you move to?
Nourish	What will be your go-to nourishment to round off your ritual?

###

Summary: Daily Practices for Your Spirit

Over the past eight days you've been working with practices and interventions that promote spirituality and self-awareness. Keep using the following daily practices to ensure you're on track:

- Simple meditation

- Inner guidance

- Authentically you

- Choose love over fear

- Choosing to help others

- Reflection

- Mental toolkit

- Morning mindset ritual

CREATING EVEN MORE HAPPINESS FOR YOUR JOURNEY

I hope that the tools and teachings you have discovered over the past 30 days have helped you to see how Now Is Your Chance to make the most of your moments and to choose to seize the day. Right back at the beginning of the book I mentioned being bullied when I was 11 years old, struggling with my sense of self and not claiming my place in the world. Now, I've found my strength and I'm helping so many of you to find yours. Allow the Now Is Your Chance message to empower you to claim your own place in the world, without having to wait a few decades to do it.

I used to think that being positive was all there is. Now, I realize that it's not about ignoring the negative – what we resist persists – but more about getting the fullest out of all of our life's experiences. It's about integrating the pain with the positive, and resolving the conflict, to allow us to feel happy and fulfilled and whole. If I didn't have my hard times, I wouldn't have been able to appreciate so deeply what's good.

My ability and capacity to help others has deepened as a result of what I've learned through my own experience, where I am able to understand and connect with the trauma and negatives that are all too common in our lives. I want you to know that the strength we have within us is more than enough to tackle anything that life throws. In adversity it's amazing how the spirit emerges and grows.

As you reflect on your 30-day journey, I ask that you ask yourself the following questions:

- What did you love about the past 30 days? Which were the tools that powerfully stood out for you?

- What challenged you or brought up resistance for you?

- Which of the tools and practices will you be taking forwards into your life with you?

Integrating these new practices into your life as habits provides both a challenge and an opportunity. Anybody can test something out – the real growth comes as you assimilate the tools and concepts in this book, so they become part of who you are and how you do.

I know that by making our happiness our priority, through working on ourselves, we are able to enjoy each step our of time here in this life. When seeking to live your happiest life, you can see that gratitude and growth are key to your fulfilment. Through greater conscious choice and awareness, you're able to see every experience as both a learning and a blessing. With the help of positive psychology, commitment and really connecting inwards with yourself, you can overcome any obstacle, whether big or small, real or imagined, and move forwards to find deep and lasting happiness, confidence, success and fulfilment.

If you're ready to take this journey a step further and work together to create your happiest life, then you should come and join me for the Now Is Your Chance Happiness Academy, my signature online happiness course, which supports you in creating transformational results within yourself, your life, your career, your business and your relationships.

Consider your biggest takeaway that you have received from reading this book. My intention is that you use *Now Is Your Chance* as a tool book to help you as you move forwards in your journey of happiness and growth. Come back to it when you feel you need a boost and understand that the tools shared here are timeless.

Take this book and run with it, share it to heal pain and promote happiness, to help you to learn and rapidly grow. Apply the tools and live them. Use them in your life, your relationships, and your career and business, and come back to them when you need to use them again. They're yours for life now. Happiness is available for you. Now Is Your Chance to choose it.

With Gratitude, and of course in loving memory of the great Louise Hay,

Niyc xx

Connect with me

 www.niycpidgeon.com

 Niyc Pidgeon

 @niycpidge

 Niyc Pidgeon

 @niycpidge

REFERENCES

Introduction

1. Gilbert, D. *Stumbling on Happiness* (Vintage, 2006)

2. http://huffingtonpost.com/gobankingrates/why-happy-people-earn-mor_b_8038640.html; accessed 27 June 2017

3. www.sciencedaily.com/releases/2006/11/061108103655.htm; accessed 27 June 2017

4. www.psychologytoday.com/articles/201307/what-happy-people-do-differently; accessed 27 June 2017

5. Burchard, B. *High Performance Habits, How Extraordinary People Become That Way* (Hay House, 2017)

6. Lyubomirsky, S. (2008). *The How of Happiness: A Scientific Approach to Getting the Life You Want* (Penguin Press, 2008)

7. Epigenetics is the study of chemical tags on DNA that switch genes on and off over time. For example, practising good health behaviour can cause chemical modification in your genes, and alter your biological processes to support better health for you and generations after you; https://www.whatisepigenetics.com/fundamentals/; accessed 27 June 2017

Day 1

1. Emmon, A. & McCullough, M. 'Counting blessings versus burdens: An experimental investigation of gratitude and subjective well-being in daily life', *Journal of Personality and Social Psychology*, 2003; 84 (2), 377–89

2. Algoe, S., Gable, S. & Maisel, N. 'It's the little things: Everyday gratitude as a booster shot for romantic relationships', *Personal Relationships*, 2010; 17: 217–33

3. Hill, P., Allemand, M. & Roberts, B. 'Examining the pathways between gratitude and self-rated physical health across adulthood', *Personality and Individual Differences*, 2013; 54(1), 92–6: DOI: 10.1016/j.paid.2012.08.011

4. Wood, A., John Maltby, J. & Gillett, R. *et al.* 'The role of gratitude in the development of social support, stress, and depression: Two longitudinal studies', *Journal of Research in Personality*, 2008; 42: 854–71

5. www.ncbi.nlm.nih.gov/pmc/articles/PMC1693418/pdf/15347528. pdf

6. Kong, F., Ding, K. & Zhao, J. 'The relationships among gratitude, self-esteem, social support and life satisfaction among undergraduate students', *Journal of Happiness Studies*, 2015; 16(2): 477–89

7. Froha, T. & Kashdanb, K. *et al.* 'Who benefits the most from a gratitude intervention in children and adolescents? Examining positive affect as a moderator', *Journal of Positive Psychology*, 2009; 4(5): 408–22

Day 2

1. Coldwell, J., Pike, A. & Dunn, J. 'Household chaos – links with parenting and child behaviour', *J Child Psychol Psychiatry*, 2006; 47(11): 1116–22

2. Leeds, L. & Hargreaves, I. 'The psychological consequences of childbirth', *Journal of Reproductive and Infant Psychology*, 2008; 26(2):108–22; http://dx.doi.org/10.1080/02646830701688299

3. McMains, S. & Kastner, S. 'Interactions of top-down and bottom-up mechanisms in human visual cortex', *J. Neurosci.* 2011; 31(2): 587–97; doi: 10.1523/JNEUROSCI.3766–10.2011

4. Feng shui is closely linked to Taoism and is a philosophical system of harmonizing energy in your environment by the placement of objects around the home

Day 3

1. http://blogs.discovermagazine.com/d-brief/2013/12/30/ body-atlas-reveals-where-we-feel-happiness-and-shame/#. WUu2ZhPyuV6; accessed 27 June 2017

2. Fredrickson, B. 'What good are positive emotions?' *Review of General Psychology*, 1998; 2(3): 300

Day 4

1. Seligman, M. & Csikszentmihalyi, M. 'Positive Psychology: An Introduction', *American Psychologist*, 2000; 55(1): 5–14

2. Hefferon, K. & Mutrie, N. 'Physical activity as a "stellar" positive psychology intervention', *The Oxford Handbook of Exercise Psychology* (Oxford Press, 2012); DOI: 10.1093/ oxfordhb/9780195394313.013.0007

3. Cotman, C., Berchtold, N. & Christie, L. 'Exercise builds brain health: key roles of growth factor cascades and inflammation', *Trends Neurosci.* 2007; 30(9): 464–72

4. Yau, S., Gil-Mohapel, J. & Christie, B. *et al.* 'Physical exercise-induced adult neurogenesis: a good strategy to prevent cognitive decline in neurodegenerative diseases?' *BioMed Research International*, 2014; doi: 10.1155/2014/403120

5. Rothman, R. & Baumann, M. 'Neurochemical mechanisms of phentermine and fenfluramine: Therapeutic and adverse effects', *Drug Development Research*, 2000; 51(2): 52–65; doi: 10.1002/1098–2299(200010)51:2<52::AID-DDR2>3.0.CO;2-H

Day 5

1. http://www.otago.ac.nz/psychology/otago057493.pdf; accessed 28 June 2017

2. Graham, T. *The Happiness Diet* (Rodale Books; Reprint edition 11 Dec. 2012)

Day 9

1. https://psychcentral.com/blog/archives/2010/05/21/the-power-of-forgiveness/; accessed 27 June 2017

Day 10

1. www.ted.com/talks/carol_dweck_the_power_of_believing_that_ you_can_improve; accessed 28 June 2017

2. Blackwell, L., Trezsniewski, K. & Dweck, C. 'Implicit theories of intelligence predict achievement across an adolescent transition: a longitudinal study and an intervention', Child Dev, 2007; 78(1): 246–63

Day 11

1. https://faithhopeandpsychology.wordpress.com/2012/03/02/80-of-thoughts-are-negative-95-are-repetitive/; accessed 27 June 2017

2. Taylor, S., Abramowitz, J.S., McKay, D., Calamari, J.E., Sookman, D., Kyrios, M., Wilhelm, S. & Carmin, C. (2006) 'Do dysfunctional beliefs play a role in all types of obsessive-compulsive disorder?' *Journal of Anxiety Disorders*, 20(1), 85–97.

Day 12

1. www.virgin.com/richard-branson/bad-decision-better-no-decision; accessed 28 June 2007

2. Land, S. & Jonassen, D. *Theoretical Foundations of Learning Environments* (Routledge, 2012)

3. Rath, T. & Conchie, B. *Strengths Based Leadership* (Gallup Press, 2008)

4. Isen, A. 'An Influence of Positive Affect on Decision Making in Complex Situations: Theoretical Issues With Practical Implications', *Consumer Psychology*, 2001; 11(2): 75–85

Day 13

1. Maxwell, J. *How Successful People Grow: 15 Ways to Get Ahead in Life* (Center Street, 2014).

2. https://internal.psychology.illinois.edu/~ediener/Documents/ Diener_1984.pdf; accessed 28 June 2017

3. Baumeister, R., Campbell, J. & Kreuger, J. *et al.* 'Does high self-esteem cause better performance, interpersonal success, happiness, or healthier lifestyles?' *Psychol Sci Public Interest*, 2003; 4(1): 1–44; doi: 10.1111/1529-1006.01431

4. Bandura, A. 'The reconstrual of "free will" from the agentic perspective of social cognitive theory.' In J. Baer, J.C. Kaufman & R.F. Baumeister (eds.), *Are We Free? Psychology and Free Will* (Oxford University Press, 2008); 86–127

Day 14

1. Csikszentmihaly, M. *Creativity: The Psychology of Discovery and Invention* (Harper Perennial, 2011. Reprint edition 6 Aug 2013)

Day 15

1. http://huffingtonpost.com/srinivasan-pillay/is-there-scientific-evide_b_175189.html; accessed 28 June 2017

Day 16

1. www.paulekman.com/wp-content/uploads/2013/07/Emotional-And-Conversational-Nonverbal-Signals.pdf; accessed 3 July 2017
2. Achor, S. *The Happiness Advantage* (Virgin Books, 2010)

Day 17

1. Wong, P. 'Meaning therapy: An integrative and positive existential psychotherapy', *Journal of Contemporary Psychotherapy*, 2010; 40(2): 85–99

Day 18

1. Sharot, T. *The Optimism Bias: Why We're Wired to Look on the Bright Side* (Robinson, 2012)

Day 20

1. Pretty, J., Peacock, J. & Sellens, M. *et al.* 'The mental and physical health outcomes of green exercise', *Int J Environ Health Res.* 2005 Oct; 15(5): 319–37
2. Mackay. G. & Neill, J. 'The effect of "green exercise" on state anxiety and the role of exercise duration, intensity, and greenness: A quasi-experimental study', *Psychology of Sport and Exercise*, 2010; 11(3), 238–45; doi:10.1016/j.psychsport.2010.01.002

Day 21

1. Fredrickson, B. 'What good are positive emotions?' *Review of General Psychology*, 1998; 2(3): 300

Part III Introduction

1. www.positiveinsights.co.uk/articles/EMPIRICAL_RESULT_OF_INTERVENTIONS.pdf; accessed 28 June 2017

Day 23

1. www.psychologytoday.com/blog/feeling-it/201309/20-scientific-reasons-start-meditating-today; accessed 28 June 2017

2. Lyubomirsky, S., Dickerhoof, R. & Boehm, J. *et al.* 'Becoming happier takes both a will and a proper way: Two experimental longitudinal interventions to boost well-being', *Emotion*; 11(2), 2011: 391–402; http://dx.doi.org/10.1037/a0022575

Day 25

1. www.biomedsearch.com/article/role-authenticity-in-healthy-psychological/95844662.html; accessed 28 June 2017

2. www.ted.com/talks/brene_brown_on_vulnerability); accessed 28 June 2017

Day 27

1. http://sonjalyubomirsky.com/wp-content/themes/sonja lyubomirsky/papers/LDinpressb.pdf; accessed 28 June 2017

2. Boehm *et al.*, 2008

3. Lyubomirsky, S. *The How of Happiness: A scientific approach to getting the life you want* (Penguin Press, 2008)

4. https://pdfs.semanticscholar.org/1bc0/e16d8b9269ee3 ca375fac97d327e6c567c7d.pdf; accessed 28 June 2017

Day 29

1. Meredith, L. *et al.*, 'Promoting psychological resilience in the US Military', *Rand Health Quarterly*, 2011; 1(2): 2

2. http://corstone.org/wp-content/uploads/2015/05/Psychological-Resilience-Positive-Emotions-and-Successful-Adaptation-to-Stress-in-Later-Life.pdf; accessed 28 June 2017

3. https://www.ncbi.nlm.nih.gov/pmc/articles/PMC3126102/; accessed 28 June 2017

4. Henricksen, A. & Stephens, C. 'Enhancing Activities and Positive Practices Inventory (HAPPI), *J Happiness Stud*, 2013; 14: 81–98 DOI 10.1007/s10902-011-9317-z (Published online: 11 January 2012 Ó Springer Science+Business Media B.V. 2012)

5. Ivtzan, I. *et al. Second Wave Positive Psychology; Embracing the Dark Side of Life* (Routledge, 2015)

6. https://thepsychologist.bps.org.uk/volume-25/edition-11/what-doesnt-kill-us; accessed 3 July 2017

7. http://www.katehefferon.com/wp-content/uploads/2010/07/PSYCH_2012123/3117240538-3.pdf; accessed 3 July 2017

8. http://psycnet.apa.org/journals/cap/56/3/28; accessed 3 July 2017

ABOUT THE AUTHOR

Niyc Pidgeon, MSc, BSc, CTLLS, IPPA, CHPC is a positive psychologist and success coach who is on a mission to help a million women change their lives through her mindset and business coaching programmes. She proudly travels the world speaking, coaching, and helping women to create more joy, personal power, and unstoppable success within themselves and their businesses.

Niyc has been appointed as a Supporting Partner at United Nations Women UK and as an Ambassador for their Onebracelet campaign to end violence against women. She spent a week masterminding with Sir Richard Branson on his private island, Necker, for the first ever women's entrepreneurship retreat there. She regularly speaks on stage in front of large audiences, in places including Hollywood, Amsterdam, Miami, London, Dallas and Sydney.

Niyc is the founder and creator of the following programs:

- Unstoppable Success Accelerator
- Unstoppable Success Online
- Now Is Your Chance Happiness Academy
- Happy Women Make More Money
- Now Is Your Chance VIP Society

She is originally from Newcastle upon Tyne in the UK, where she won Young Business Person of the Year in 2015, and currently lives in Los Angeles.

www.niycpidgeon.com

HAY HOUSE

Look within

Join the conversation about latest products,
events, exclusive offers and more.

f Hay House UK

🐦 @HayHouseUK

📷 @hayhouseuk

❤️ healyourlife.com

We'd love to hear from you!